Happiness is...

...Heaven Made Marriages

Happiness is...

...Heaven Made Marriages

Compiled by LaJoyce Martin

WORD AFLAME PRESS
8855 Dunn Road • Hazelwood, Mo. 63042

Happiness Is. . .
Heaven-Made Marriages

By LaJoyce Martin

©1985 Word Aflame® Press
Hazelwood, Mo. 63042

ISBN 0-912315-86-5

Cover Design by Tim Agnew

Scripture quotations in this book are from the King James Version.

Printed in the United States of America.

Dedicated To
my
"Dream-Come-True"
from
Your Flowersy Girl

Contents

Contents

Preface

. . .And they lived happily **even** after. That is the ending of a perfect romance story.

God must have loved romance. The Bible is full of it. He even lets us in on how some of the couples in the Good Book met!

•Remember the Benjamites that hid in the vineyard? Each man picked a wife from the dancing Shiloh girls, grabbed her, and ran home again. That was some way to get a wife!

•And how Ruth met Boaz? He was her employer!

•And how Esther married her Prince Charming? In a contest, she won his heart by simplicity and a beautiful spirit.

•And how Rebecca wed Isaac? Talk about a Lonely Hearts Club! A third party was their match-maker.

•It was love at first sight for poor Jacob when he saw Rachel at the well. He kissed her before the first date.

•And then God gave us His own love story—an autobiography, the Song of Solomon, the greatest love story ever written.

"Heaven-Made Marriages," a rare collection of "How We Met" stories written by ministers and their wives, has been swelling in my heart like leaven for more than a year. But it took a special friend like Sister Dolores Neely to give me the nudge I needed to put it into print. She is one of the most romantic ladies I have ever known, and through her hard work and faithful backing, you have "our" book.

On these pages, you will find a delightful variety of love stories, written by young and old, for your reading enjoyment. They will entertain you, thrill you, uplift you. . .you might even shed a tear now and then. You will know when you close the book that these are *"Heaven-made marriages."* The ones who lived happily *even* after. . . .

Happiness is. . .

. . .a thirty-day test

By Melissa A. Anderson

"Who does he remind you of?" my girlfriend asked as we watched a tall, "older" man being baptized. I quickly responded by naming a former young man that I had dated. We had no knowledge of the man who was baptized, but we thought he could be related to Brother and Sister J. W. Gilstrap, who were holding a revival at our church in Buchanan, Michigan.

After the revival services had ended, our Pastor kept in touch with the "older" man and helped him through a brief illness. Later the man moved into the home of a young couple in the church so that he could attend church regularly.

The tall, "older" man was George W. Anderson, and he was not that "old." In fact, after the experience of the Holy Ghost and the new life he started living, he was quite an "attraction" to all the single girls in the area—especially the ones past twenty-five and who were in fear of being an old maid. Many of the people started immediately to find him a wife but he wasn't really interested in dating the first several months he was in church. Busy getting adjusted to a whole new life that had opened to him, he walked carefully and prayerfully with God, avoiding any activity that might bring a reproach upon these wonderful people and the new way of life he had discovered. Later he did accept several blind dates, not wanting to hurt the feelings of the people in their effort to match him with someone.

George was boarding with my girlfriend's brother, who lived two or three doors from where I was rooming and boarding with my girlfriend's family. Many times we did not have a way to church, and George was thoughtful about seeing that we had a ride. When the young people began teasing me about George, it made me "turn him off," as I couldn't stand to be teased. Besides, I had my mind made up about what kind of a husband I wanted and he certainly did not fill the bill!

In the first place, he was ten years older than I. Secondly, although he was a very good carpenter and held a very good job for that time, I wasn't interested in a carpenter. I planned to marry a preacher or an evangelist. Then, among other qualifications, my future husband had to have a better education, be an intellectual, and be musically inclined. I had definite "guidelines" as to just the kind of person I would marry.

George became involved in activities of the church; he worked on the building program, offered his car to take a load of young people to rallies, and participated actively in the worship services. Although he was shy about testifying in church, he became a real witness on the job to the men with whom he worked. He easily hurdled the "persecutions" and the attempts to change him to other doctrines. For a time I served as youth leader, but I was amazed when I learned that George wanted to speak for a youth service! Little did I know that God had called him to preach the night he received the Holy Ghost. Fearful and overwhelmed with knowing that he had received a call into the ministry, he wanted to make an effort to begin. The first night he spoke, his tall frame quivered as he gripped the small pulpit desk. His voice was so soft that he could hardly be heard two rows back. At this point it didn't seem that he was anywhere near being a preacher!

As time went on, we were together a lot in groups, but I could tell he really liked me. He told me later that he especially noticed me when I was a bridesmaid in my cousin's wedding. I still would not consider dating him, however, since I never was the kind to lead a man on and hurt him. I wouldn't date anyone unless I really liked him. I tried to find George other girls and consistently refused his attention. And yet I was drawn to him and realized he needed someone—someone to whom he could talk, and who could help him get adjusted to the Pentecostal way. He had never been one to attend church, he had never read a Bible, and he was like a foreigner among the Pentecostals. But he had an intense desire to do what was right.

After the first year, he decided he wanted to date and to find a wife. I refused to date him and deliberately avoided any situations that would end up that way. When my mother came to visit me, he wanted to take us out for dinner. I refused, but much to my horror my mother said, "Sure, I'll go." I tried to convince her that I didn't want to date him, and that she could not go without me. But she liked him. She was also the kind of person who was outgoing and who "mothered" everybody. So George ended up taking us out to dinner, and later to other places in the area that were points of interest. Mom really liked him. Unknown to me, she told him that as far as she was concerned he could marry me if he could win me!

Since I had resisted all of his efforts, he turned to dating others. Well, this was something different! I was used to having his attention and being "first" with him. When he dated my girlfriend and she evidently enjoyed his company, it made me think a bit more about him.

Although he was dating others, he let me know that I was his "first" choice. When he took me to the train as I left to go home to Iowa from Christmas, I gave him a tie that I had purchased for his new brown suit. When I returned, he gave me a music box that played, "O Promise Me." Later I found out that he had gotten five girls a Christmas gift—an unavoidable situation that he had gotten into, he explained!

While at home, I talked about George with my mother. I told of his kissing me once (and I cried. . .could you believe?) and how I really didn't know how I felt about him. Although he wasn't the man in many ways that I thought I wanted, yet he was nice and good and seemed completely in love with me. He had begged me to date him steadily for thirty days, and then if I didn't want to continue, I could quit. I was such a frustration to him; he said he had never had trouble getting a girlfriend, but had always had trouble getting rid of them! Mother told me to go ahead with the "thirty-day test," and I took her advice.

On New Year's Eve of 1949, we had our first date of the "thirty-day test." We sat together in church services, had dinner dates, and spent time together almost every day. On February 2, he asked me to marry him. My answer? "I don't know." Almost every date he continued to ask me to marry him, and I continued to say "I don't know"—until June. Then I accepted and agreed to announce our engagement in the newspaper; however, I stipulated that if I felt it was not the Lord's will I would back out on the plans.

George and I were married on September 16, 1950. Thirty-five years later, I can look back and see that God had it all planned and that George Anderson coming into my life and sharing it was the best thing that could have happened to me. George has often encouraged me in doing the will of God, and he has been good to me and for me. The "thirty-day test" proved to be the turning point in my life!

Our Wedding picture, September 16, 1950

Mom and my husband.

Thirty-two years of marriage, 1982.

Happiness is. . .

. . .a surprise merry-go-round wreck

By Kathy Bailey

W hat a place to pick a husband! On the *elementary school* playground!

Had we been six-year-olds, this would not be unusual, but seventeen-year-olds playing on the kiddie playground?

Sharing our "mature" pastime was my best friend, Donna, and her boyfriend. It was a beautiful evening in May.

Donna and I were idly pushing ourselves around the merry-go-round, discussing all those earth-shaking world events that all teenage girls discuss. My "husband-to-be" (he wasn't aware of that fact yet) decided that we were much too leisurely in our endeavor to have fun, and that we would benefit from a faster ride, which he provided.

This certainly caught me by surprise! As we were flying round and round, I lost my hand grip and slipped off the seat, but my foot caught as I was falling. So for two rounds I was seated, only on the ground.

For the next three or four weeks, it was impossible to forget Bill everytime I sat down! I was bruised from my knees to my waist!

Bill expressed such deep remorse about this and showed so much loving compassion that it made all the pain bearable! I knew then I had found the one-in-a-million guy!

My husband-to-be and I were not in the church when we met and dated. I was reared in the Methodist church and Bill was a backslidden Pentecostal. Bill's brother, Terry, had started dating Donna, and we usually went double, even marrying within six months of each other.

Our favorite pastime was mountain climbing (they were actually just large hills!) around our hometown. We spent considerable time searching for historical Indian lookouts and other points of interest important in bygone eras. We would then have long discussions on what probably happened there. It was a fun and inexpensive way to spend a Saturday.

On Friday nights, we followed the time-worn ritual of the other high-schoolers, "dragging" in Terry's '57 Chevy. Our orbit led from Sonic Drive-In down Main Street to the Gay Nineties Ice Cream Parlor, making a turnaround in their parking lot, and retracing the route back to Sonic. . .over and over again. Sweet monotony! We burned up a lot of gasoline, but it was "the thing" then.

Since neither Bill nor I had a car, we would sometimes borrow my grandparents' car or my mother's car, repaying their loan with a free car wash on Sunday. Not a bad trade to be able to get out for awhile!

By fall, we had become quite fond of each other. For my birthday in October, Bill surprised me with a promise ring. He paid for it on the installment plan. It was white gold with two diamond chips, and I was thrilled with Bill's romantic sweetness.

June of 1971 was a momentous month. Bill got his first car, a two-door, red and white Impala Chevrolet. It was everything a young man could want. It was perfect! We spent endless hours washing and polishing that "baby." It was his pride and joy!

I also got my first car—a 1960 blue-green Rambler. It ran, but it also smoked and drank. I always felt sorry for whoever was behind me in the fog.

It seemed that a lot of exciting things were happening. This same month, Bill landed a very good paying job with a construction company. We were into "high money" then. The menu on our dates changed from hamburger to steaks! We spent a lot of time together now.

Little did we know that that summer was going to change our lives drastically!

On Sunday, June 18, Bill and I went to Sunday school and were persuaded by the teacher of the youth class to stay for church. The conviction of the Lord was so strong in that service that I wasn't sure what to do. A sister in the church came back and invited me to the altar. I started to go when Bill grabbed my arm and said, "Let's get out of here!" I followed him out.

As we were leaving the church, we decided to go to

Ft. Worth for lunch. After eating, we went to play miniature golf. I still remember the game. He won. By that time, the conviction I felt had worn off and we had a fun-filled afternoon.

I had gotten a job through the school's Vocational Office Education program working for a veterinarian, starting in my junior year and continuing until I was graduated.

Tuesday morning, July 20, 1971: Bill drove to work late and parked his car crooked because there wasn't enough time to park it straight. That was the last thing he would remember for days.

Just before noon that day, his boss thought it looked like rain, so he told Bill and another employee to move a piece of plywood to cover the pier hole they were drilling. Unaware that there was already a seventy-three foot pier hole underneath, Bill took two steps and fell into the cavity.

Terry was working for the same crew and it took several men to hold him back; this was a terrible ordeal for him.

Sure that Bill was dead, they finally found someone to go down by crane to retrieve the body. They tied a rope under his arms, and had lifted him about fifteen feet when the rope slipped and Bill hit bottom again. But this time, he started moaning and they knew he was alive.

He was rushed to St. Paul's Hospital in Dallas where a team of thirteen specialists pronounced him hopeless.

I was devastated! Here was the fun-loving guy that I was crazy about in Intensive Care Unit in critical condition. My mind somersaulted back to the times he had run across the sand at the beach acting like a motorcycle and doing crazy stunts—and here they were talking about amputating his legs below his knees.

He was in a coma and did not even know I was there! I would go into ICU, tell him I loved him, and leave crying. I was only allowed to stay five minutes at a time, but I drove a hundred and twenty miles round trip just to spend those precious five minutes with the guy I loved.

His injuries were unfathomable. He had crushed both feet and ankles, both legs were broken (one in two places), he suffered a broken collar bone, crushed ribs, and a collapsed lung. He also had two compression fractures of the back, a jaw broken in four places, and a concussion. God was the only answer!

Coming out of the coma, Bill slowly regained his memory. When he first recognized his mother, he kissed her on the hand and cried because he remembered who she was. He wasn't the only one crying in that hospital room that day!

Two weeks, many miracles, and many surgeries after his accident, Bill asked everyone to leave the room because he wanted to talk to me alone. "Kathy," he said, "I love you and I want to marry you, but I want you to know I'm going back to church." I didn't understand it all at that time, but I knew we would stick together.

Friday, August 13, 1971: Bill was released from the hospital just three weeks after his horrible accident. That was our lucky day!

"When I first saw you, I wouldn't have given a plug nickel for your life, but the Lord wanted you to live for some reason!" one of his doctors told him.

True to Bill's promise, we started to church in September. We attended the United Pentecostal Church in Cleburne where Brother B. E. Moore pastored. On

September 8, Bill received the Holy Ghost in his wheelchair, and on September 11, I was baptized with the Holy Ghost, too. Now we were starting our lives over the right way!

The next year was full of ups and downs—and many surgeries. But we finally decided to set a date for our "big day." Bill was walking again with the assistance of army combat boots for ankle support. Picture him in our wedding in his black tuxedo, pink shirt. . .and combat boots. "I was prepared for the battle!" he has always teased me. The date was July 22, 1972, exactly one year and two days after his accident.

Amidst candles and flowers, pink-frocked bridesmaids and handsome groomsmen in their tuxedos, our wedding was a dream come true!

Down the aisle I came in my white lace gown with its six-foot train. I was to be given away by my brother. Instead of exchanging rings, Bill and I had a special sonnet to quote to each other. I was to go first, and he was to respond with his. But he was so nervous that he said his first, and so fast that I could hardly understand him. We were able to laugh about this later.

Very much in love and very happy, we set up housekeeping in Cleburne after our honeymoon trip to Austin, San Marcus, and Waco.

My birthday was coming up and there was no money for a present. I had to leave for work early and was the first one up. On the morning of my birthday, I arose to a whole house full of signs and notes, telling me how much I was loved and wishing me a happy birthday. . .in the bathroom. . .in the kitchen. . .in the closet. . .and even on the steering wheel of my car. I've had many birthdays since, but no birthday has ever put me "on top of the world" and given me the warm feeling that that one did. That feeling has lasted many years!

Our first child, Amy Catherine, was born in August of 1975. She was the most beautiful child in the world (and still is!).

When Amy was one year old, I started to nursing school, and with the help of my precious husband, I eventually graduated as president of my nursing class. I was able to share my joy with the special people I went to school with.

Our life was not easy, but we were happy. We faced yet another crisis in 1978. Bill was working for the Johnson County Sheriff's Department as a crime scene investigator. He went with a deputy to serve some civil papers, and was involved in an automobile accident enroute. An eighteen wheeler truck hit their car in the side and Bill suffered another compression fracture. He spent another seventeen pain-filled days in the hospital. The Lord was dealing with Bill about the ministry and he was fighting it.

Three months after this accident, while Bill was standing in a healing line, the Lord told the minister who was preaching that if Bill would accept what God had for him, He would completely heal his back. My husband answered, "Yes, Lord! I'll preach Your Word!" He has not had any back problems since that night.

When I married Bill, I never dreamed that I would be a preacher's wife. It took some getting used to. I wasn't sure what to do, what to say, or how to act! But I was willing to follow my mate wherever he led.

We started out by helping the pastor of our home

church, Brother F. L. Ashley, as youth ministers. Bill preached and we sang at *many, many* nursing home services. We have many sweet memories from this work.

In December of 1979, we were blessed with our second child, a boy. We now had our "million dollar family." But all was not well. Tiny Eric Marshall was born a month prematurely and had Hylane Membrane Disease; his lungs were not properly developed. When he was three hours old, he was transferred to the Ft. Worth Children's Hospital into the Neonatal Intensive Care Unit.

Before Eric was born, Bill kept saying he did not know how he could ever love another child as much as he loved Amy. This, in fact, really seemed to bother him. But after sitting for countless hours in a waiting room, washing and robing just to touch our newborn son, I remembered his fears. "Do you love Eric any less than Amy?" I asked him. He was made to realize that he did not have to *divide* his love. . .it grows and multiplies!

We went into home missions work in Jacksboro, Texas, early in 1980. The Lord blessed our work, and we had built the little Sunday school to a high of thirty. But Bill could not find a job in Jacksboro, and was forced to drive eighty miles to find employment. He was unable to hold up to the physical stress. Testing showed that one kidney was not functioning and the other was already one-third gone. This required yet another surgery to remove one kidney and repair the other.

The night before the surgery was a trying time for both of us. Nervousness and uncertainty overwhelmed us. I reached for the Bible and read one of the Psalms until the peace of the Lord filled us and the room we were in. *"How do people of this world face problems without the Lord to lean on?"* I asked myself.

We moved to Johnson City, Texas in July of 1982. The Lord has blessed us with a beautiful church and a great group of people here!

I catch myself thinking, *"You know, sometimes you look over your life and you see many disappointments and valleys, but there are always mountain tops, and many, many times of joy. It seems to be easy to love someone when the times are good. . .when the bills get paid and everyone is healthy and happy. But it's those times when everything goes wrong. . .when there's hardly any money at all. . .when everything you touch breaks or goes out. . .when you have to pull yourself up by the bootstraps just to get up in the morning. . .it's those times you know what love really is. You know then you've got that special person God meant just for you. All the flowers, special notes, anniversary trips. . .are icing on a special cake."*

We've been married for more than a dozen years now and my first instincts—out on the elementary school playground—were right. Bill's love and compassion have never changed, either for me or for the souls he helps along the way. I found a one-in-a-million guy, and I'm thankful I found him *first!*

Our Wedding, 1972.

Bill holds Amy for the first time.

To the prom we go, 1970.

Our family.

Happiness is. . .

. . .to Margie from Cleveland

By Margie Becton

Standing in Kress' five and dime store, I looked up at the clerk and asked, "Could you write 'To Cleveland from Margie' on that large chocolate heart?"

"Is this Cleveland a little blue-eyed, blond-headed boy?" she asked.

"Yes," I nodded.

"He was just in here and ordered one 'To Margie from Cleveland'!" she said.

In my eight-year-old mind, it was the city's largest store. Two little people, thinking of each other with a young and tender friendship, had chosen the same store to select their purchases for Valentine's Day.

From then on, giving each other something chocolate with white frosting writing on it became a seasonal tradition with us.

Early memories include the excitement of attending church and the eight-mile, thirty-minute car drive that was a time of family fun. Our destination was the First Pentecostal Church, better known as "Fifth and Victory," Little Rock Arkansas, one block from the state's beautiful capitol.

God arranged the Dyson family so that the first four children were well-spaced from the last two. The two older children had begun dating and had a car of their own, making the passenger load to church perfectly even. Because of the church's ideal location, most of our friends either walked or rode the city trolley.

One friend in particular was always there early. His older brother waited for my older brother—and the blue-eyed, blond-headed boy (my folks called him tow-headed) was waiting for me. Bad weather, bad roads, flooded areas, or our rural chores such as milking cows, a new litter of kittens, puppies or pigs, occasionally threw us behind schedule. Being late was a sad experience for me; I would miss seeing my little friend who was sound asleep on his pallet under the bench by the time song service ended! I would stay sad until the next service. After more than fifty years, I still find it exciting to be in church with my now greyish-blond haired friend and husband.

Starting to school was an ecstatic experience, but by afternoon I became depressed. I missed my nap and worried about my mother being alone during the day. I wished desperately that she had someone to keep her company.

In the third grade it happened. My family moved to the city, leaving our country home in the custody of relatives. Having children in grammar, junior high, and high schools, my father rented a comfortable home just blocks from all the schools. . .and within walking distance of Jim and Christine Becton, their closest friends. Now I could go to school *and* church with my blue-eyed, blond-headed friend! We ate lunch together, played games before and after school, roller skated, rode bicycles. "Anne Over," chalk the rabbit, hopscotch, tug of war, marbles, and jacks were games we shared with neighborhood children.

One afternoon I came home to a baby brother. Little Paul David was a dream come true, and we affectionately called this brown-eyed, red-headed boy, "Buzz," the name he bears to this day.

February's severe weather curtailed our outside games. Baby-sitting Buzz occupied my time. My friend Cleveland was intrigued by our player piano, placing his fingers on the keys that bobbed up and down as he pumped vigorously. It also fascinated the baby.

Saturdays and Sundays were fun times; many hours were spent playing indoor games at our house or the Bectons. My two oldest brothers, LaFayette and Charles, worked at the Little Rock Furniture Company where our father was a foreman for more than thirty years. Both Cleveland and I had a brother named John and after World War II, my brother John joined Charles in the Dyson Furniture Factory.

We moved back to the country for a brief two years, then back to the city again. Moving about the town became a fad for the Dysons and Bectons, and since duplex living was the "in" thing, our families chose this new method of housing just a few blocks apart. My mother's sister, Adline, lived on the other side of us, and a sister, Birdie, just a block away, making a convenient setting for the birth of my baby sister, Marilyn Ruth.

About this time, my friend Cleveland got an accordion which took up a lot of his time while my new sister, with her fiery red hair, bright blue eyes, and late evening colic that produced lusty crying, took up mine. This soon passed, however, along with the school year. Grammar school days slipped by and all too soon a move back to the country separated my best friend and me, except for church services and frequent family get-togethers.

The ride with my father and his carpool from our country home to the city school would have made for a long day except for the thrill of going to my aunt's before and after school, making it possible to walk to and from school with Cleveland. We often met our friends, Billie J. Carmickel and Buddy Corbin. Four friends walked home together; these four friends became two couples several years later.

"Moron" jokes were quite the thing and we never had time enough walking home from school to tell them all. My older brothers had shared a new one with me, and prayer time at church found Cleveland and me on our knees telling "one." And guess who caught us not praying? Our pastor's wife, Mrs. G. H. Brown! We made a vow, out of fear, never to tell each other another "moron" joke!

A few days later, I got out of school early and my friend walked me to the bus stop. Climbing up on a high brick pillar, he looked down at me with those sparkling blue eyes. "I have something to tell you, but you may not like it," he said. He had a mischievous look in his eyes.

"Oh, no! No more 'moron' jokes!" I said, shaking my head.

"It's not a joke," he said, "I love you." He jumped down and ran a half city block before looking back.

I was never the same again. The words reverberated over and over in my mind: *To Margie—I love you—from Cleveland.*

For some time I had been teaching him the good manners a boy should show for a girl. At the restaurant (drug store in our case), he should pull her chair out for her. He should take her coat, open doors for her, walk on the curbside for her protection, tip her elbow at the corner or curb, and other gentlemanly gestures. These I had learned from a seventeen-year-old boy who recently moved to our city and attended our church with his aunt.

"I'll help you get a girlfriend if you'll learn to be mannerly," I told Cleveland, little realizing I was training my own suitor.

Three years of my five-year diary was filled when it occurred to me that friend Cleveland had helped himself to reading it while visiting in my home. One embarrassing entry said, "John Becton held my hand at church tonight." Really, it was a lengthy handshake in the foyer, but after all, what is an imagination for?

High school days hastened by, especially for me since I took my junior and senior year in one, attending summer school to complete my credits. Cleveland and I were in different schools our senior year; he graduated from Little Rock Central and I from Mabelvale High. His baccalaureate was on Sunday afternoon and mine on Sunday evening, posing no problems for us to be at each other's services. Graduation was equally as simple; he graduated one evening and I the next. Where to now?

We were sixteen and our paths were separating again. Cleveland spent the summer teaching in Dallas Stamps-Baxter School of Music, and in the fall of 1945, enrolled in the Pentecostal Bible Institute of Tupelo, Mississippi.

I went to work for my father in the upholstering department of the Little Rock Furniture Company. My brother John and his childhood sweetheart eloped. My father shrugged his shoulders and said, "Oh, well, that's kids for you. Probably won't be long until Margie runs off with some little tow-headed boy."

Christine Becton picked that right up and said, "I wouldn't call my son a little tow-headed boy!"

My father just blushed and walked away.

My friend in Bible school grew up physically and spiritually during the year spent there. He received his call into the ministry, and wrote many interesting things in his two-paragraph, one-page letters. I did a lot of reading between the lines. . .to *Margie from Cleveland.*

In late summer of 1946, Cleveland Becton and Rexie Wilcox finished a revival and were in town for a few days. They came by the factory to pick me up after work. Right there on the sidewalk, in broad open daylight, and with Rexie's face shining, I was presented an engagement ring!

Our plans for the future were made in snatches as I was never alone with my life-time friend until our wedding night some fifteen months later. He was a "minister of the gospel" and a full-time evangelist, so to be dating alone was a no-no even though we were engaged to be married. We had to have a chaperone at all times.

At summer's end, 1947, Cleveland asked my father if we could set a wedding date. My father immediately said yes, but my mother protested that I was too young. "Take all the advice you can get and then do what you please," my father insisted. With that profound statement, we made our plans to marry on October 22, 1947.

The home church was in revival with Reverend Andrew D. Urshan during the month of October, so arrangements were made to take one night off for the wedding. Reverend Urshan lit our candles and gave a beautiful talk on marriage just before our pastor, Reverend G. H. Brown, performed the ceremony. Brother Urshan also gave us a "special" marriage certificate to go along with our marriage license. Our pastor and church friends bade us Godspeed.

"I'll see you two at 9 A.M. for prayer meeting in the morning," Brother Urshan said.

"Yes, sir," we replied.

To Margie: We will continue our honeymoon in Dallas, Texas at General Conference. Tomorrow we go to church at 9 A.M.—From Cleveland.

Margie Dyson and Cleveland Becton—Married October 20, 1947

> *Three Children:*
>> *Rudy Cleveland—Born October 15, 1948*
>> *Ronald McKelvy—Born September 2, 1952*
>> *Margie Renee—Born February 28, 1958*
>
> *Four Grandchildren:*
>> *Alicia Christine, Arlen Rudy, Jared Austin, and*
>>> *Richard Chad*
>
> *Churches Pastored:*
>> *Bay City, Texas*
>> *North Little Rock, Arkansas*
>> *Nashville, Tennessee*

Reverend Cleveland M. Becton—General Secretary-Treasurer of the United Pentecostal Church International.

Walking home from Junior High graduation: Billy Carmichael, Buddy Corbin, Margie Dyson and Cleveland Becton.

Our Wedding

The Wedding Party

The Becton family: Top row, lt. to rt. Renee and Rick Flowers, Helen and Rudy Becton, Cheryl and Ron Becton. Bottom row: lt. to rt. Arlen Becton, Rev. and Mrs. Cleveland Becton, Alicia Becton.

Happiness is. . .

. . .tender memories of wedding a Bell

By Charla Bell

"I will love, honor, cherish, leaving all others, cleave only to thee, in all things true and faithful, given to the other for richer or poorer, for better or worse, in sickness and in health; till death do we part."

Eight years and ten months after Raymond and I made these vows, our orange and white Toyota Corolla was headed west on Interstate 20 outside of Shreveport, Louisiana. It was a colorful fall October 26, Sunday afternoon. A happy family of four were on their way to a preaching engagement for that night. Our small eighteen-month-old baby girl Karen, and our five-year-old son Paul, were in the back seat playing. I was reading the real estate section from the *Shreveport Times.* Monday we planned to look for a home.

Suddenly our car started flipping (five times it rolled). "What is happening? Am I dead or alive? Where is my husband? . . .my baby?" Paul was trapped in the car with me and black smoke was coming from the motor. I hear screams, "Hurry, get the people out of the car! It's going to catch on fire."

A man under the influence of alcohol, traveling at the rate of speed approximately one hundred miles per hour, had struck our car from the rear.

At approximately 7:30 p.m. the doctor stepped to my bedside at Schumpert Hospital in Shreveport, Louisiana, took me by the hand, swallowed hard, and as if it were the hardest words he had ever uttered, said, "I'm sorry Mrs. Bell. We did all we could, but your husband is gone."

"Oh, no! no! gone? gone!" I could not grasp his word *gone!* So final.

"I will love, honor, cherish. . .till death do us part."

I remember my first encounter with Raymond. We were at Texas District Camp Meeting in Lufkin, Texas. It was a beautiful, bright, hot, sunshiny East Texas Tuesday afternoon. I was talking with several girls under the big water tower that stands in the center of the campus. Raymond walked up with one of his boyfriends, whom I knew, and this friend introduced us. I remember how handsome he was, dressed in a gold-colored sport coat, yellow shirt, dark pants and a gold comb in his pocket. His hair was perfect and the blackest black I had ever seen. There was a special quality about him. I noticed he had an unusual depth of maturity. He spoke of his recent graduation and plans for going to college. This meant that I was a year older than he since I had graduated the year before. He was extremely nice and a real gentleman, but I didn't think about dating him. He offered to buy us all a coke. I made sure I didn't walk by him to the concession stand. We talked and laughed as young people do; then we left to get ready for the evening service.

Later that evening, a girlfriend and I were standing in front of the huge tabernacle. Out of thousands of people, who should come along but that good looking Raymond Bell and a boyfriend of his! They started talking to us and asked if they could sit with us during the evening service. The four of us went inside and Raymond found his place next to me.

That night after church we went out to eat. The next day we were together and I spotted my mother on the big camp ground. Most people would not have trouble pro-nouncing the name Bell, but when you have just met your future husband, whose name is Raymond Bell, you are just not responsible for what you might say. There's a lump in your throat, butterflies in your stomach, and you feel like you're walking on clouds. I introduced Raymond to my mother as Raymond *Ball*.

He was quick to correct me, "No—*Bell*."

"Oh excuse me, yes. *Bell*."

He and his family left on Thursday. There was cer-tainly a tender place in our hearts for each other. His mom told me later that as they drove home Raymond was very quiet and his sister teased, "Yeah, Raymond, it's different now, isn't it?"

Brenda, Raymond's sister, had cried when she left

Jimmy, her steady boyfriend who later became her husband, at home. Raymond had teased, "That's silly, I would never cry over a girl." Now there were tears in his eyes as they drove home to Gladewater, Texas.

How could two people be so much in love already? God had surely brought us together. It was a special love. A love that would last "till death do we part."

I went to my home in Hillsboro, Texas, and Raymond was in Gladewater, Texas one hundred and forty miles apart. The next day the phone rang. Yes, it was Raymond. My heart skipped two or three beats, and when I hung up the phone, I felt like I could conquer the world. No boy had ever affected me like this one!

The first letter I received from my love, he wrote: "It happens to be one of my faults not to be able to express myself in words, but with all sincerity I am truly *missing* you. Nevertheless, maybe if nothing happens, I can come to Hillsboro to see you in two or three weeks."

Who could wait two or three weeks? Later in the week, I received another phone call: "Would it be possible for us to get together this weekend?"

"Would it be possible?" I thought.

Saturday evening finally arrived and when I opened the door and saw that sweet darling standing there, once again my heart was in my throat! We both were smiling a shy smile. Was this for real? Was he really sitting in my living room?

It was good to be together, and we enjoyed every minute. Sunday evening Raymond suggested we go for a little drive before he returned home. We drove to Waco, Texas, which is about thirty-five miles from Hillsboro. We drove through Cameron Park. The scenery was beautiful.

We stopped the car and walked over to a big rock fence. From the summit we could look deep into the valley of the Brazos where tall cottonwoods fringed the big river. This is known as Lovers' Leap.

The scenery was not only breathtaking, but while we were standing there, somehow Raymond's hand and mine unconsciously entwined. A little thing, but it was wonderful and our hands just seemed to fit together so well. I wanted to keep those moments forever.

Again, parting was sad. We said goodbye and promised to write each other.

During the week, a beautiful bouquet arrived at my house from Raymond. He was upset because he had ordered roses and gladiolus were delivered.

The letters and calls did come frequently. The money he was saving for a new car went to Southwestern Bell Telephone. He settled for a used car rather than the new Ford he had ordered. He would tell his family, "Oh, but that girl is worth every penny I spend!"

I was planning on going to Texas Bible College in Houston, Texas, and Raymond was going to Kilgore Junior College, but when September came, we were both off to Texas Bible College. We were not together much since the rules allowed only one legal date a month and that was with a chaperone. Besides, between work and school, it was hard to get together.

Our annual General Church Conference was in New Orleans, Louisiana the last of October. Both of our families would be there, so we decided to go on the weekend. A girlfriend of ours was riding in the front seat with us and one of the T.B.C. deans was riding in the back seat.

When we got to New Orleans, Raymond and I

dropped our passengers at the Conference auditorium and went alone to get something to eat. When we got back to the school campus, we were put on restriction for breaking school rules.

Togetherness makes your love grow or causes a couple to drift apart. When two people love each other as much as Raymond and I did, a wedding cannot be far away. We really did love each other and did not want to wait for the June honeymoon.

We decided to get married December 30, while we were out of school for the Christmas holidays.

I went home to make arrangements for the wedding. So much to do and so little time to do it in! Wedding dress, sewing, shopping, invitations, flowers, showers and the list continued.

A few days before we were married, I was working at the job I had before I went to school—helping during the Christmas rush. A customer complimented my hair, and asked, "How long is it?" With my mind on the wedding, I said, "Only ten more days!"

Every letter was a countdown—"Only 20, 19, 18. . .more days until you will be mine. I can hardly wait to see you—wish we were getting married sooner. I love you more everyday. Without you my life would be incomplete."

The last letter I received from Raymond, he wrote:

"I can hardly wait to see you. You just don't know how lonesome it is without you—but someday it won't be like this; you'll be with me all the time.

"It sure was good to hear your sweet voice again last night, Honey! It was so hard to tell you 'bye. You mean

everything to me. I'm so thankful the Lord brought us together.

"I wish there were words which express how much I love you. I have never been happier in all my life than I am since we are engaged."

December 30 finally arrived—our wedding day and also Raymond's nineteenth birthday.

Under the soft glow of candle light, we clearly and confidently exchanged vows: "I will love, honor, cherish—till death do we part."

We said goodbye to our families and drove to Waco, Texas. We had a steak at a nice restaurant. While we were waiting for our food, Raymond excused himself and went to the pay phone and called my mother. "Just wanted to let you know we made it to our destination fine." What a way to win a mother-in-law's love!

Raymond had made reservations at a motel, but he couldn't remember the name of the motel! A look in the phone book jogged him to his senses. We checked in the bridal suite as Mr. and Mrs. Raymond Bell. I had already practiced writing my new name over and over, weeks even months prior.

Three years after our marriage and after graduation from Texas Bible College, Raymond felt his call into the ministry. I remember the struggle for God's will in his life. Finally it was,

"Perfect submission, all is at rest
I in my Savior am happy and blessed
Watching and waiting, looking above
Filled with His goodness, lost in His love."

One Sunday night, Raymond stood in the congregation of Spring Branch Calvary Tabernacle Church in Houston, Texas. Tears were rolling down his face as he quoted the verse of Scripture, Isaiah 6:8: "Whom shall I send, and who will go for us? Then said I, Here am I; send me."

We evangelized after graduation from Texas Bible College. During this time, our first child was born. After four years of marriage God blessed us with the sweetest, loving, blue-eyed baby boy, whom we named Paul. How happy we were! He was our little valentine, born shortly after Valentine's Day on February 15.

We were later called to Aransas Pass, Texas, where we pastored our first church. While there, God blessed us again with a child, a darling little girl. Just what we ordered—first a boy, then a girl. Karen was our Easter bunny. She was born on April 11, and we brought her home from the hospital on Easter Sunday. Her daddy was about to pop the buttons off his coat! His family was his heartbeat. Often he would say, "I'm so proud of my little family."

After we were in Aransas Pass a little over three years, we moved to St. Louis, Missouri, for a few short months. Here Raymond was trained to manage the new Word Aflame Bookstore that was soon to open in Bossier City, Louisiana.

We loved it in Louisiana. Raymond assisted Reverend L. J. McDaniel, pastor of the United Pentecostal Church of Bossier City, and also managed the Word Aflame Bookstore.

It was a busy life between work, church, bus ministry, and Sunday school, yet Raymond still had time for his family.

I remember the little things we did as a family that brought so much happiness.

Some evenings we would walk to Baskin Robbins for an ice cream treat. We would push Karen in her stroller and sometimes let Paul ride his small bicycle.

The children loved to ride their daddy's horse, which was his knee. As he tossed them in the air, there were squeals and giggles. Oh, the laughter and warmth of home! Sometimes Paul and Karen would be on the floor with daddy tossing them in the air; then he gave them a ride on his back.

Sometimes when I was cleaning house, I would find a note that Raymond had left me on the dresser. It might read: "Darling, I will miss you today and will be glad to be with you this evening." On other days, the telephone would ring and I would hear Raymond's voice on the other end: "Hi, I just wanted to hear your sweet voice."

He would often stop by the store and bring me some small something—a book, magazine, or candy, and say, "I've been thinking about you." Once he engraved a small inexpensive trophy that read:

World's Best Wife
Charla Bell

A small thing, but it said "I love you" in a big way.

Our last weekend together was just as special as our first weekend.

Friday evening about 3:00 p.m., there was that special knock at the back glass-sliding door of our apartment on Preston Street in Bossier City, Louisiana. Karen, our little eighteen-month-old baby, had also learned her daddy's special knock and ran toward the door jabbering, "Da-da."

I opened the door and Raymond handed me a box of millionaire candy, kissed me and was on his way.

Saturday night we went to a new shopping mall that had just recently opened in Shreveport, Louisiana. It was such an enjoyable evening, all four of us together. We walked hand in hand, talking, smiling, and watching our little ones have fun.

Sunday morning Raymond helped dress Paul, and I dressed Karen for church. A kind lady at the church remarked when we arrived, "What a lovely little family!" After church we went out to eat with our pastor and his wife.

Raymond had a speaking engagement that evening at a church about seventy-five miles from Bossier. We rushed home, dressed for the evening service, and we were on our way.

I carried the newspaper with me to read the real estate section on the way. Monday we would look for us a house.

Raymond was always kind, fun, and special, and to-day was no exception. We talked about our future, laughed, and smiled at each other.

It was about 2:20 p.m. Our little Toyota wheels rolled on. Then a crash, flipping, screams, smoke, cries, blood, ambulance.

He's *gone.*

"I will love thee. . .till death do we part."

Charla Bell and family.

Happiness is. . .

. . .being stranded in a snowstorm

By JoAnn Berry

I could hardly wait to get back from our Colorado honeymoon to "my little girl!"

Bobby's first wife had died, leaving him with a baby daughter. Kimberly was two and a half years old when I got her.

Maybe I identified with the motherless child. I was from a broken home, adopted by a paternal uncle at thirteen months of age. *"Kim will never feel like a stepchild,"* I promised myself. *"She's mine. . .as much mine as any child I give birth to in the future. God just gave her to me in a different manner."*

51

Cupid's tiny arrow found its way into my heart in August of 1969 at the Amarillo Camp Meeting. I had drawn a picture in my youthful mind of my dream man and poof! Here he was! Hadn't I prayed for a tall, dark, and handsome evangelist with black hair and brown eyes and here he stood in front of me? I mean, after all. . .God promised us the desires of our hearts!

Doubts crowded my mind. This handsome young preacher from Oklahoma was grieving for his late wife— and I was only a school girl of sixteen!

"You're so starry-eyed, you're embarrassing us!" some of my friends told me.

"He's so far out of my reach!" I thought, crying my heart out with confusion. *"It would surely take a miracle of God for this dream man to be mine!"*

In the months following the passing of his wife, Bobby kept a diary, often writing down his feelings and thoughts. Many of these had no relevance to him at the time. He had never met me personally, heard of me, nor did he know that I even existed. He wrote that he felt directed to "West Texas" and "the Dumas church" and had recurring thoughts of "a little orphan girl." He was puzzled by these thoughts. He asked himself: *"Is Kimberly going to be an orphan?"* And if so, *"How would her becoming an orphan tie in with West Texas? With Dumas? Is it possible that I will lose my own life in West Texas, leaving my precious child fatherless also?"*

The camp meeting closed on a black note for me. . .that is, until I learned that my pastor, Brother Frank Martin, had asked Bobby to come to Dumas and preach that weekend. It must be noted that Bobby's sister, LaJoyce Martin, was my pastor's daughter-in-law, and rumors have it that this well-known matchmaker added her bit of spice to this new development. She was at Dumas at the time. Their car was broken down, awaiting repairs.

Eagerly I anticipated Sunday services. *"I can just sit and feast my eyes on him without suspicion during church,"* I thought. *"Because, after all, you're supposed to pay attention to the preacher!"* But of all days, it was my turn to teach children's church during morning worship that weekend. Of *all* days! I tried to find a substitute to take my place, but no one had mercy on me! I was, however, granted the privilege of parading the children right in front of him on the way to children's church. I could glance sideways and see him at close range! But alas, by the time I got near where he was sitting, I was too nervous to look up! I had blown my chance!

"Now my problem is how to teach these children this morning and listen to him preach at the same time!" I reasoned. So I would get the children busy and slip away to the door near the platform. . .and stay as long as I dared, peeking through the crack in the door and listening intently. His subject was, "God's Divine Purpose and Will For Your life."

I had on a very simple black dress and wore my hair up which gave me a look of maturity well past my years. He never dreamed I was only sixteen! He was twenty-nine.

"Who was the young lady in charge of children's church?" he asked his sister that afternoon.

To his surprise, she replied, "Oh, she's a little orphan girl a family in the church has taken to raise."

This caused strange, disturbing thoughts in his mind. . .Dumas church. . .orphan girl. Into the wee hours of the morning, he still wrestled with unanswered questions. Finally, he cried out, "Oh, Lord, if it's Your will, *You* work it out!" and dropped off to a restful sleep.

The "God, if it's Your will" entailed a whole week of Bobby helping overhaul the Elroy Martins' car motor *three* times—only to find nothing amiss in the motor the last time they tore it apart.

Friday night was a fellowship meeting at our church. Brother Brian, missionary from Australia, was our speaker that night. He felt so sorry for the Martins and their lame car that he *prayed* for it that night! The next day it started miraculously.

I was in charge of the soda and coffee after the service. Bobby, who seldom drank anything after church, suddenly developed an unquenchable thirst for Cokes! Did he feel the same electric charge I felt every time our hands touched in the passing of a drink? And how was I to know he would make himself miserable from eating too many of my peanut butter cookies? And since *I* made them, can you imagine my joy when he bought all the rest of them!

When Bobby returned to Oklahoma, my heart went with him. My adoptive parents were uneasy about my feelings for him, fearing heartbreak for me. I was a country girl, reared in poverty. They felt I would never stand a chance with the high-flying evangelist driving the white Lincoln Continental. But when my mother tried to discourage me, I was undaunted. "This one's mine, Mother!" I said simply. "I'll take the chance of getting my heart broken!"

Bobby showed Kimberly my picture when he arrived home. "Mommy!" she exclaimed joyfully the first time she saw it, and begged to see the photo often. She would scribble little love notes to me on the bottom of Bobby's frequent letters, saying, "I writtin' to Mommy! I *wuv* Mommy!"

My next goal was to get to the National Conference in St. Louis to see him once again. I had never ventured far from our small shotgun house by the railroad—and certainly had never stayed in a motel or eaten out! *"Surely $50 will be adequate for my expenses!"* I thought. I made plans to sell my sewing machine, one of my few earthly possessions, to negotiate this amount, but my parents helped me to come up with the inadequate funds.

I rode with my pastor and wife and roomed with two other girls. I ran out of money the second day! However, "my" evangelist from Oklahoma saw to it that I didn't starve! (Not that I needed much to eat, as excited as I was!) And on this trip, I got to see "my baby girl" for the first time!

During the holidays, Bobby's sister invited me to go to Oklahoma for Christmas with them. It took lots of persuasion to get Mom and Dad's consent for the three-day trip. But it was worth the coaxing. The moon and stars beamed their blessings on our quiet reunion as we strolled along hand in hand through the sleepy little town of Morris that Christmas Eve.

The next morning, the ground was covered with ten inches of the most beautiful white, fluffy snow that I had ever seen! And guess who got the blame for praying in the winter storm?

"Mother and Daddy will never believe this!" was my first thought. *"But it'll surely melt off so that we can get home on schedule."*

However, with each moderation came a new freeze, followed by yet another snowstorm. We were snowbound for a glorious week of sledding, snow-ball fighting, and ice skating!

The perfect moment came on Christmas night when

Bobby proposed to me. I had no idea my heart could contain such happiness!

As soon as we got back to my folks, Bobby asked their permission to marry me. They were not surprised. They gave us their blessings. "We'd rather that you marry young and get a good man," they said, burdened with the knowledge of my real mother's seven broken marriages, my father's multiple failures at wedlock, and countless other divorces in the family which, for a lifetime, had tormented my young mind. "The difference is, we have *God* directing our lives," Bobby said, erasing the misgivings I had about my infamous family history. Bobby went with Mother to check me out of school.

We planned a March, 1970, wedding. Although it was a short and beautiful courtship, it was the longest three months of my life. Time snailed by and seemed to stop.

One unspoken cloud marred my sunshine. That was the fear of rejection by Kimberly's maternal grandparents, the McFarlins. *"Will they accept me? How will they feel about me mothering the child of their only daughter?"*

My fears were soon assuaged when I received a kind letter from them shortly after we announced our engagement. "Because of your loss of parents as a child and our loss of our daughter, we can help each other," Sister McFarlin wrote. "You will be as a daughter to us and we will be as parents to you." After that, I was no longer apprehensive, and eagerly awaited meeting them.

Inquiries were made concerning my needs of household items for a local wedding shower. "I don't know what all *he* may have, but I'll write and ask what we will need," I said.

"You mean, you would use something that *she* had

used?" someone asked tactlessly.

I was shocked by the question. "Of course! Why not?"

"Well, *I* wouldn't touch anything *she* touched!"

"I don't look at things that way at all! We can't throw away all those nice furnishings and buy everything new just because *she* touched them! Must we throw away his shirts because *she* ironed them? Shall I not touch the baby *she* held? No! I refuse to be that way!" I could not imagine anyone being so pettish.

Although we were very poor, I was determined to have a nice wedding with beautiful memories. So I borrowed a wedding dress from one friend, a veil from another, and got my shoes at a garage sale. The flowers were magnificent Kleenex carnations! The cake was donated and Bobby decorated it himself.

As our courtship neared the end, Bobby (who was poetic and romantic) wrote: "You are my sunshine when skies are gray. . .you are my oasis – on a barren desert. . .you are my happiness – when sorrow has been my lot. . .You are my hope – when all seemed hopeless . . .You have watered our relationship with enough tears of concern to bring into existence knowledge of the deep sincerity of your love. – And for 'these' the world has no supplement – therefore you mean *more* than all the world to me, Darling."

When I met Bobby at the altar on our wedding day and said "I Do," I not only became his wife, but I became a mother. Being a "child bride" of sixteen, I felt my childhood "make believe" husband had come to life and my favorite doll was now a real live one. I was beside myself with delight and felt like God had just given me a slice of heaven!

"Did you marry me *just* for Kimberly?" Bobby has asked me teasingly since that day.

I have kept the promise I made to myself fifteen years ago. Kimberly and I have always been close to each other. We "grew up together." She is now a beautiful seventeen-year-old, and I share her joys and her tears. I seldom go anywhere without her. She is as completely my own as the three "other" children God has blessed Bobby and me with.

An excerpt from his last letter summed up our hopes and dreams for the future:

"Though this is the ending of a beautiful courtship – our real romance is just beginning. . .An entire life-time of the moon shining softly upon two lovers' faces nestled closely together – in love, forever. . .an eternal honeymoon – if 'we' want to make it such."

And we do!

The Last of Miss JoAnn Jordan

(Written by Bobby Berry, 1970)

A true story of the sudden disappearance of a small West Texas village girl.

Preface

Out of the past comes tales of the sudden disappearance of a villager who returns occasionally, only as a ghost. Our minds draw us away from the possible authenticity of such a tale because of the mental limit of human possibilities and reasoning.

In this true story, the incident that took place on the

21st of March and the young Miss JoAnn Jordan's disappearance was attributed to a great power possessed by a young Oklahoma minister.

* * *

JoAnn, a young, petite, brown haired girl, was often seen in the stores and on the streets of Sunray—a little village in the panhandle of Texas. Seemingly she was an ordinary young lady amongst the townfolk with the exception she had often attended a church of a rather strange and spiritual group since she was a child. Could this possibly be some clue relating to her sudden disappearance? There is, I would think, a reasonable possibility considering some earlier events that have taken place in and about the church and its surroundings.

It was noticed, by at least a small group of this congregation some few months ago, that a rather noticeable change was transpiring in the life of the young member. Some became alarmed and concerned at what they saw, and the transformation they witnessed caused more questions to arise, only to be answered in the days and weeks to come. The question that remained unanswered for months are now being answered in the minds of most, due to several spectacular events that took place in more recent weeks and days.

JoAnn Jordan will remain in her hometown village only as a ghost. Her name, JoAnn Jordan, which is well established and remembered about the small West Texas community, will only be used from now on by the villagers to establish proper identity among themselves of that young Miss Jordan—that used to be.

On the very night she was whisked away and suddenly dispatched to the realms of another world, she seemed inclined to an intense state of emotion, though not at all in the slightest state of depression, but rather a highly exhilarated state of mind.

It was witnessed by many responsible and reliable adults, and since the night of that unforgettable incident, the news spread across several states.

It seems that something somewhat similar to a great white phantom was seen just before and at the time of her disappearance. A young preacher, reportedly from Oklahoma, was the last one seen in her company. From reports and witnesses, we learned his name was Bobby Berry.

Could it be that this young minister of the same faith of religion as she, had somehow cast a spell over the young lady with sufficient psychic power to allure our little Miss from her community, her church, and her friends, and leave us with only a memory of her? Beyond argument of cultured skeptics, this is inevitable, for from now on and into the eternal future there will never be known or seen, walking the streets of her hometown village, a well-remembered young lady, Miss JoAnn Jordan.

For the night that the preacher accompanied her and that great white phantom appeared and took her away, she was transformed in a simple yet dignified manner and suddenly became Mrs. Bobby Berry.

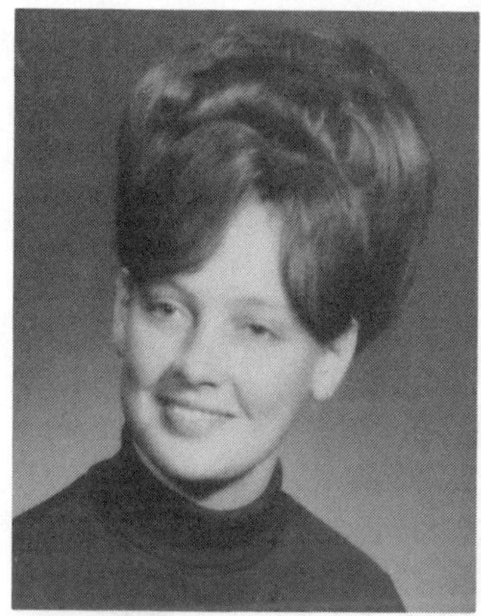

My "engagement" picture—taken when Bobby checked me out of school.

Dreams come true, March 21, 1969.

My first meeting with my little girl, October 1969.

Our whole family: Kim, Kenyon, Kendall, and Krisha.

Happiness is. . .

. . .a knot tied by a barefoot preacher

By Lorene Berry

"I'll have to rock J. Deane to sleep before I can go with you, Donald," I told him on our first date. J. Deane was my baby brother, the last of Mama's dozen children. I was seventeen when he was born, and had cared for him like a young mother, changing him and fixing bottles, as well as rocking him to sleep.

In asking me to go with him, Donald, in his timidity, mumbled, "Everyone else is already gone!"

"Is he insinuating that I'm the last straw for him?" I wondered to myself.

We double-dated with a couple of friends who had

just started dating themselves. The four of us went to a "picture show" in Meridian, Texas, ten miles from our hometown of Walnut Springs. Our transportation was a 1925 Model T touring car with the top let back. It was a nippy mid-November evening—rather cold in an "air-conditioned" car! The movie was "silent," with conversation flashing on the screen to be read.

All during the summer, I had attended Saturday night parties at the homes of various friends. Frequently we made candy, each furnishing an ingredient. The boys picked out the pecans; Donald was one of those boys.

"Let's play 'Wolf over the River' or 'Pleased or Displeased' " were common suggestions for games. When cold weather set in, however, we moved inside and the dancing began.

Donald never learned to dance; he was a musician, providing music for the dancers. Therefore, I never cared for dancing. We made an agreement that if there was any drinking, or questionable conduct, we would disband and go home. At one such party, a lady playfully told Donald's "fortune." She painted my picture very plainly as his future bride.

For Christmas that year, Donald gave me a miniature cedar chest filled with stationery. I still have the memoir.

In the summer of 1932, I attended an outdoor "Holy Roller" revival one Sunday night. Such conviction seized me that I promised myself, *"I won't go back again until next Sunday night."*

But on Thursday afternoon, July 21, at a cottage prayer meeting, two of my cousins received the Holy Ghost. My older sister came home and excitedly reported: "Avo and Howard prayed through!"

"I'll just have to go tonight to see how they act!" I thought.

I could not stay out of the altar. By eleven o'clock, I had received the Holy Ghost and was a "Holy Roller," too.

After church, Donald walked me home as usual, but our words were few and far between. He was listening breathlessly for me to tell him that I would not date him any more since he was a "sinner."

The next night found *him* at the altar. He did not receive the Holy Ghost that night, but he went to the cottage prayer meeting Saturday morning and was filled with the Spirit there.

"I was afraid I'd lose you," he said later.

Several of our old partying friends got in the church. Twenty-seven of us were baptized on Sunday, including my mother and his. It was Mama's forty-seventh birthday.

The Civilian Conservation Corps recruiting officers came through our small city enlisting young men. Since Donald was out of work and times were hard, he decided to join up for a year or so. The truck was due to leave soon. Donald slipped away to my house to tell me goodbye, and when he returned, the truck was gone. They had left him behind!

Donald caught a ride to Meridian, thinking to overtake the truck, but alas, they had already left there also. Later, we saw the great hand of God in it all. None of the boys who went knew the Lord in any measure, and Donald was just a "babe in the Lord." He probably could not have survived spiritually.

Our lifestyle changed, but our courtship continued. We walked to and from church, stopping on moonshiny summer nights to sit on a large white rock about fifty yards from my house.

One of our friends put sideboards on his truck, stacked benches in it, and transported us for miles around to revival meetings. Each of us would pay 10¢ for the gasoline. This beat the movies by a million miles! We saw multitudes of souls saved.

We seldom dated alone. Donald had no car, but he borrowed one now and then. On such occasions, we would sit in the car when we came in from church. But if Mama thought I was staying out too late, she would call me to come in. She kept a careful watch over her seven girls, for which I have always been very thankful.

In early summer of 1933, Donald asked my parents for my hand in marriage. I was twenty-one.

"Times are awful hard, Donald," Mama said. The Great Depression held the nation in its deathly grip, and Donald had no car, no suit, and no job!

With a lot of faith and a borrowed dollar, we went to our pastor's house on June 23, 1933, to be pronounced man and wife. He wasn't home; he had gone fishing. We waited. . .and waited. . .and waited. He showed up around 10 p.m., and kept us waiting no longer.

On his front lawn, in his fishing clothes and in his sock feet, he performed our marriage. He tied a good knot, one that has not slipped in over fifty years.

We moved in with Donald's parents. He helped his dad in the blacksmith shop for a short duration. Then God opened up a place for us rent-free and Donald landed a job with the Works Progress Administration (W.P.A.) at a whopping 70¢ a day.

Certainly our marriage was made in heaven and ordained of God. He blessed our home with two wonderful children, both in the work of God, and seven lovely grandchildren.

Donald was called to preach, and our pastorates took us to several locations in Texas, Oklahoma, and Arkansas. He served on the District Board in all these states.

God has blessed me with exceptional health. I've never been hospitalized in my entire life, or even been on medication. I still have my natural teeth! All praise goes to Jesus.

In December of 1981, we retired in the same small community where we fell in love with each other and the Lord.

We celebrated fifty wonderful years together in July of 1983. We have lived a rich, full life in the work of God. I could not have asked for a more satisfying life—such contentment, peace and happiness. A life spent in God's work is very gratifying.

My husband composes his own valentines to me, and this is an excerpt from a favorite of mine that he wrote in 1980:

The Sweetest Valentine

We've weathered the time thru tears and joy,
And I hope I'm still your "brown-eyed boy."
You don't have to wonder about me, dear,
'Cause my love grows stronger every year.

Tho your hair has turned to "silver gray,"
I still love you the same today.
I took your hand in a wedding vow,

And it's just too late to change me now.

My mind goes back when you wore your frock
And sat many nights on that "Big White Rock";
Then the golden moon seemed so divine,
That's when you began to be my Valentine.

I'm just plain poor with not much to give,
But my heart is yours as long as I live.
I was looking for a treasure with lots of worth
When I found you somewhere on this earth.

I remember well, way back down the line,
When we swung together on the "old grapevine";
Things have changed, but not this heart of
    mine—
You're still to me, "The Sweetest Valentine"!

Just me, honey!
D.F.B.

I LOVE YOU

When you and I were young, "Reenie."

Happiness is. . .

. . .an overseas pen pal

By Rose Carter

"*What fun it would be to have a pen pal stationed in Okinawa!*" I thought. However, marriage was the far-thest thing from my young mind. I was going to enjoy life and see the world before I settled down!

My girlfriend was married to Douglas Carter's buddy and I started corresponding with him through them. He was in the army and I was in high school.

We wrote for almost a year before Doug got a thirty-day leave. He decided to come to Austin, Texas, and visit his friend. Besides, he wanted to meet this girl named Rose Flandermeyer. With a name like that, he *had* to see what

71

she looked like!

I was working at Taco Bell, standing at the counter, when this young man with porkchop sideburns and a mustache walked in and introduced himself as Douglas Carter. We met after I got off work. . .and this started our courtship.

He stayed in Austin during the Christmas holidays, and before he left for Georgia where he was to be stationed, I was wearing his promise ring.

He was discharged in February of 1972, gave me an engagement ring in March, and we were married on June 10, right after I graduated from high school. There went my plans to see the world!

We were happy, young, and in love. We moved a lot, to Louisiana and back again. When we lived in Austin, we drove the 400 miles to Pineville, Louisiana, every weekend to drink and party. Our lives began to fall apart.

Ours was not an "instant" Heaven-Made Marriage. In fact, it took God quite awhile to *make* a marriage out of the mess we made of things.

Doug wanted his freedom, so I put him out on the highway with his suitcase, and as I drove back into town, I could hardly see the road for the tears. What had happened to the love we had for each other such a few months ago?

It began to rain—drops, then trickles, then torrents! *"He sure must look funny standing there soaked to the skin, packing a big suitcase,"* I thought, laughing aloud. *"He'll change his mind and come home ready to stay."*

He did return to the house, but only to put on dry clothes and take the money we had saved out of the cookie jar for a bus ticket. It wasn't funny anymore.

A week later, he called wanting to come home. "I'm sorry," he told me. "Come and get me." However, when I got to his mom's in Louisiana, he had slept off his high, didn't even remember calling me, and wanted to know why I was there. And although he returned to Austin with me, it wasn't long before he hit the road again.

The next time I saw him, he showed up at my job, as unsure of what he wanted as a child, but sure that he loved and wanted me. So I moved to Louisiana with him. *"We have it together now,"* we thought. *"A new life, a new start. . .and old friends."*

We were searching for answers and did not know where to go to find them. Our spare time (we managed to have plenty of it) was filled with drinking and smoking pot. I spent more and more time home alone while Doug was "out with the boys." I seldom knew where he was. When he did come home, he was so drunk or spaced out on drugs that he didn't remember driving home.

I worried a lot. Maybe he had a wreck? Got in a fight? Was locked up in jail?

I did not realize that he had a drug problem in the service before I married him. He failed to tell me of the many times he almost overdosed on acid and heroin overseas. And here he was heading down the same road again!

In the next few tortuous months, Doug miraculously escaped death many times. He began dealing heavily in drugs, buying pot by the pound instead of by the lid. We even grew the stuff in our back yard! Our neighbor's brother was a narcotics agent and why we never got caught is still a mystery.

An old buddy named Sydney showed up in Doug's

life—unfortunately. Doug began taking things from the house and selling them without my knowledge—first a bed, then my sewing machine. He used this money on his mad craving for drugs; often there was no food in the house. A friend of Doug's worked at the Pizza Place in town, and Doug did manage to bring home the leftovers from the restaurant.

I would soon be giving birth to our first child. Doug and Sydney took off to New Orleans for off-shore work. Sydney had "connections," but it wasn't with a job. They narrowly escaped being pulled into the underworld. With their dirty long hair and beards, they were unable to obtain employment. They stood in front of a fast food store, begging money from customers to return home.

When they got back, they stole my ten-speed bicycle and traded it for seven grams of angel dust. . .and decided to make a living fishing. Doug went to the store and took a package of weiners without paying for them, with the intentions of taking them to the river. The alert clerk jumped from behind the counter shouting, "I got you!" A scared Doug threw the weiners at the clerk and ran. In his haste, Doug wrecked the car on his way back to the fishing hole. In their stupor, they imagined that they were cave men, making primitive sounds that disturbed the other campers. Terrified, they hid in the car all night— and brought home no fish.

Doug was at the end of his rope—and so was I. I had hoped that the birth of our daughter, Michelle, would solve our problems, but *she* could not make him love me and get off drugs.

He sat at the table in tears, writing a letter to me. "I can't tell you how I feel," he said. So he wrote: "I'm sorry and no good and can't ever be the husband you deserve." He just didn't have the power to break the chains that had him bound!

He carried a loaded shotgun in his car. The police were aware of this and were on the alert. "They'll never get me without a fight," he told me. He planned to commit suicide.

Doug had a Pentecostal sister who was praying for us. We were separated when Sister Youngblood came by the house to invite us to a revival. Doug was there to see the baby. *"Why not go to church? After all, it couldn't hurt anything."*

There wasn't even an evangelist that night, so Doug's brother-in-law preached. Neither of us remember what he preached, but something got hold of Doug! Someone invited him to pray.

I watched as he walked down to the front, tears flowing down his face. But I wouldn't move, even when the ladies tried to pray with me. Not because I didn't want to, but because I was confused and did not understand what was happening.

When Doug got through praying, he came straight to me, held me in his arms, and said, "I'm coming home!"

There was something different in his voice. . .but could I trust him? Was this going to last or would I get hurt again? He didn't even smoke a cigarette that night!

The next night, Doug received the Holy Ghost. He had invited some of his friends to church and they didn't know how to react to this joy-filled buddy who was hugging anybody that got near! He was baptized that night and was "drunk," but this time in the Spirit.

Doug had only been in the church a week when he

heard that Sydney was in the hospital with an overdose. His father found him sitting in the middle of the bed trying to pick flowers off his bedsheet and put them into a medicine bottle.

When Doug went to see him, Sydney pointed to the next bed over. "You see that bed? It's got your name on it. I can see it!"

Doug left the hospital thanking God because that *could* have been his bed if God had not reached down just in time! Sydney had the mind of a three-year-old child.

I could see the marvelous change in Doug's life and wanted that change in my life, too. Reared in the Lutheran Church, I was steeped in tradition and God had to show me a lot about holiness that I didn't understand. But two months later, I received the Holy Ghost.

Now, twelve years later, I can truthfully say that God has taken the broken pieces and made us whole. He made a preacher out of a drug addict!

I have no doubts that God put Doug and me together in His great plan. But it took a lot of work on His part to get our story in this book. I'm so glad He didn't give up until ours, too, was a Heaven-Made Marriage!

"My pen pal."

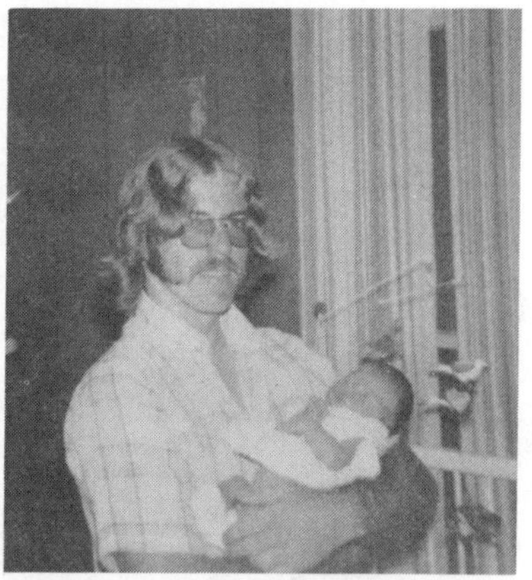

Doug holding our first child, November, 1973.

Wedding Picture, June 10, 1972.

The Douglas Carter family.

Happiness is. . .

...a familiar Bible Story

By Jack and Bobbie Courtney

Jack is the youngest of two brothers and one sister in his family. By the time he graduated from high school in Breckenridge, Texas, in 1937, his father, Jesse Courtney, was in very ill health.

Due to his father's physical condition, it was necessary for Jack to go immediately from high school graduation to a job offered him in the purchasing department of Phillips Petroleum Company.

The band and orchestra director at Breckenridge High wanted Jack to accept a scholarship (which he said he could be instrumental in acquiring for him) at Hardin-

Simmons University in Abilene, not far from Breckenridge. "You can work your way through the university by playing the violin," he said.

Jack's reply was one he has never regretted, due to the circumstance which prevailed. "I appreciate the offer of a very nice opportunity. But my father and mother need my help. I must accept the job with Phillips Petroleum Company." The job paid $143.00 per month. For a seventeen-year-old high school graduate, that was fantastic wages in 1937. There were even grown men in those days who would have been glad to get that kind of pay. To Jack, taking the job seemed to be the thing to do, under the stressful circumstance of his father's failing health.

Later years called for service with "Uncle Sam" in World War II Signal Aviation including instructing in combat communications in Fresno, California—then a voluntary stint in the China-Burma-India zone until the war's end. In retrospect, Jack said he now (as a Christian) can really relate to the verse of the song:

> *"Through many dangers, toil and snares,*
> *I have already come;*
> *T'was grace that brought me safe thus far,*
> *And grace will lead me home."*

After the war, Jack went to Longview, Texas, where his mother, brother and sister had moved. His father passed away a short time prior to his service overseas. On his deathbed in the hospital, his father told Jack, "I know I don't have long. But I'm consoled in the knowledge that I can count on you to take care of your mother. You will take care of her, won't you?"

Jack managed a reassuring smile as he gripped his father's hand and replied softly to keep his voice from breaking, "Of course, I will." A few days later, his father passed away.

Jack's brother and sister already had their families, and his father felt that Jack was the logical one to take care of the mother after his decease.

Jack and his mother moved in together after Jack was settled with a job in Longview. He could not afford a house, and for years they lived in apartments. His firm conviction was this: "I don't care how good a mother is (and mine was as good as they come) and it makes no difference how sweet a wife can be (and I got the best), but putting two women in the same kitchen won't work! Until I can afford a connecting (but separate) efficiency apartment within our home for my mother, I will not entertain the idea of marriage."

Years of work in the accounting department of an independent oil operator/producer in Longview gradually brought Jack's wages to a level that enabled him to get a home. Finally he was able to build that attached efficiency apartment for his mother, with the help of his brother-in-law (a carpenter), who built it nearly at cost.

In the meantime Jack had joined a denominational church. He became song leader, choir director, and was active in various other capacities of that church. But a dear aunt (who, incidentally, lived to be 101 years old) and her oldest daughter began fasting and praying to make Jack *miserable* until he received the Holy Ghost baptism and was baptized in water in Jesus' name! They lived 270 miles away, in Cisco, Texas, but distance was no barrier to their prayers!

Miserable! "Put *crumbs* in his bed! Put *sand* in his bed," they prayed. "Take away his appetite for food," they agonized. Talk about God answering fervent prayer! Wow! "I couldn't eat—I couldn't sleep," Jack said. "Every time I opened the Bible, the words *Holy Ghost* seemed to stand out from the page." Jack finally got a prescription of strong capsules for sleep from his doctor who said, "*This* will make you sleep!"

That night Jack kneeled by his bed and prayed, "Lord, I've gone as far as I can go. If you don't give me the Holy Ghost, just take my life before morning. I can't bear to see another sunrise without the Holy Ghost!"

He took the strong capsule for sleep and went to bed. He had no one to pray with him, or to encourage him to receive the truth. The capsule was *quite* effective! He was out like a light!

"But when God gets ready, you've gotta move," the song says. Around three o'clock in the morning, the effects of the strong capsule gave way to the mighty power of God's Spirit! "My eyes popped open like I had never closed them—and yet my body was completely rested," Jack said.

"I felt the power of God saturate my bedroom!" he exclaimed. "Every baptism of the Holy Ghost, regardless of how it appears to the recipient, is just as great as mine, but to me it seemed as though thousands of needles of gold were pouring down on me, going all through me, filling my soul with an ecstatic joy that defies my feeble attempt to describe!"

Needless to say, there was no desire or need for further sleep that night. After he praised the Lord at length in tongues, and he and the Lord had their wonderful time together, he went to his mother's bedroom, awakened her, and told her the good news. Although she had never received the Holy Ghost, she was happy for Jack and rejoiced with him! "That was the most beautiful sunrise I had ever seen," Jack exclaimed. Soon the entire family became hungry for God, and they received their baptism of the Spirit, also.

Jack related the foregoing experiences to accent the point that it was not until he sought the Lord with his whole heart that God began to direct his life. He started working things out for Jack to eventually acquire the home and the efficiency apartment for his mother, which he desired. It was then that Jack started seeking the will of God for a good, Holy Ghost-filled woman to be his wife. "Seek ye *first* the kingdom of God, and his righteousness; and all these things shall be added unto you" (Matthew 6:33).

He met a consecrated woman (in the truth) from Arkansas, and began dating her every weekend that he could. He would go on Friday night, and return home Sunday afternoon. He would attend her church on Sunday morning, and return home in time for Sunday night service at his local church.

This went on for about one and one-half years. Proposal had been made, and marriage had been discussed —but with no definite answer. Finally, Jack pressed for a definite decision. "She had foresight enough to pray earnestly for a definite answer from God," Jack said.

"She told me that she was very fond of me, and felt a definite closeness. She explained that she would even miss my visits if I chose to stop coming, but her feeling in the Spirit (after much prayer) was that it was not God's will for us to marry," Jack stated. "Instead of being sad,

I should have been glad, because later I realized what I thought was love was really only infatuation. She had foresight enough to seek God earnestly for guidance that saved both of us from a tragic mistake," he said. It really pays to find the definite will of God—especially in decisions as important as those concerning matrimony.

Not long after that, Jack began asking God about another young lady in Longview that he felt was "looking my way," he said. "I'll never forget that Saturday morning as I knelt in prayer beside my bed. I liked the lady in question, and asked God if it was His will for me to date her," he stated.

His Sunday school quarterly lessons were open on the bed where he was praying. It was open at the lesson for the next day concerning the widow and her son and Elijah, in I Kings 17.

"As I was praying about the lady friend in Longview and the Lord's will," Jack related, "suddenly I was aware of a strong presence of God's Spirit in the room. It seemed to permeate the atmosphere." Jack said his eyes seemed magnetically drawn to the open book in front of him, and to the part of the lesson in I Kings 17:10 concerning "the widow woman," and then the twelfth verse referring to her and her son.

Jack said, "It was at that moment God spoke (not audibly, but just as surely) and said, 'You will marry a widow who has a son.' That was all He said.

"It was such a surprise, I could hardly believe the short but very important message I had received from the Lord," he stated. This was beyond Jack's comprehension. He thought, "I don't even *know* a widow who has a son!" But yet there was no question in Jack's mind and heart but that this message had truly come from God.

He was so sure of it that he felt he must tell his pastor at that time, Brother D. L. Spears. "I was afraid Brother Spears would think, 'What kind of screwball do I have here?' " Jack mused. But no, on the contrary, Brother Spears was genuinely concerned, and stated he would help Jack pray about it.

Jack recalled, "Frankly, I was expecting a widow with a son to start attending my local church who would be a rank stranger." Jack was wrong again. A big surprise awaited him!

While all this was happening, Bobbie, his future wife lived in Cisco, Texas. She heard a sermon in her church (United Pentecostal Church) about the prophet Elijah. The text was in—that's right, you guessed it—I Kings 17:10-12, regarding the man of God, the *widow,* and her *son.*

After the service was dismissed, a very close friend of Bobbie's came to her and said, "Bobbie, *that* message was for *you!*"

Bobbie replied, "I know it, Grace."

Bobbie had been a widow for about five years at that time, and she was not looking for a man in her life. "But I'll let her relate how God spoke to her through the Scripture and sermon mentioned above, and the subsequent experiences leading to our wonderful marriage," Jack said.

"Let me close my part of the story," Jack stated, "by saying that I am bound by two wonderful and beautiful bonds of love—first with God, and second with the best wife in the world! You ask, 'Why the best?' You see, she was *God's* choice for me, so no one else would be close to right! *Separation* and *divorce* are two words excluded from our vocabulary because of enduring love placed deep in our hearts by God Himself!"

"What therefore God hath joined together, let no man put asunder" (Matthew 19:6).

(Jack Courtney is a lay-minister. He states that he has never felt the call to pastor or evangelize. His calling is mainly for teaching, and writing in particular.)

I was the oldest of six children in my family. We grew up in Cisco, Texas, a small town of approximately 4,500 population. We children attended the United Pentecostal Church, and I received the Holy Ghost when I was nine years old. When I look back at that time in my life, I realize this was nothing short of a miracle—considering the fact our parents *sent* us to church, although they themselves would not go with us. All the religious teaching we received was at church and Sunday school.

Reverend and Mrs. E. J. Blackwell were co-pastors of the church, and she was in charge of the pulpit ministry and was mightily used of God in preaching and teaching, as well as in the healing ministry.

Sister Blackwell performed the ceremony for me and my first husband's wedding. I was not quite twenty years old. Two years from that time, he became ill, steadily becoming worse over a span of ten years—a malady known as Wilson's disease. He finally became a complete invalid.

We had one child (a son), and he never knew what it was like not to have a sick daddy. My husband (Bill) would romp and play with our son (Terrell) until he became so ill he couldn't.

His illness progressed until finally, his father and his sister (who wasn't married) had to help me so that I could work. They attended to Bill during work days, and I would take over on weekends.

The Lord was really with us, even though I constantly was faced with doctor and medicine bills. But I am so thankful that through this long ten-year valley, I never quit paying my tithes and seeing that Terrell got to church and Sunday school. So it was really the Lord that always made a way when many times it seemed there *was* no way!

I would always tell Terrell what the doctor said about his daddy's condition. I felt that in that way he would be prepared for whatever might happen. But he would always reply, "No, Mommy, Jesus is going to heal my daddy." However, the sad day came on September 21, 1959. It was before anyone got to the house to sit up with Bill that night. Terrell and I were home. Bill peacefully went to sleep in the Lord.

It was a long valley we walked through, but the Lord was with us all the way. And now it had ended in death. Although I was left a thirty-two year old widow with a twelve-year-old son, I was not afraid. I had worked almost all my life and I had a job. And more important than that, I had a son who needed all the direction I could give him to live for the Lord.

My husband and I both knew Jack. Having many relatives in Cisco, he always spent a week vacationing there. Brother and Sister Blackwell would have him preach and teach. Once, while he was there, he came with the Blackwells to pray for Bill. Since he was a musician himself, he always encouraged Terrell to keep playing the piano.

He was kept quite busy during his visits ministering, playing the violin, singing in quartets for the services and on radio programs in Eastland, ten miles away. Everyone in the church loved Jack, and they were always glad when he came to visit.

After my husband's death, I had my house remodeled inside and outside. I was geared in my thinking to make my son happy and help him live for Jesus. My thoughts were, "I surely do not need a man! I have the Lord, and He will see us through."

Every night before we went to sleep, we would read a Bible chapter, taking turns reading a verse. It was normal procedure for us to get a carload of young people and go to youth rallies and singings at the other churches in our area.

But one day—five years later—the Lord showed me that Terrell needed a man around our house. I realized this through Terrell's frequent visits to a man's house in the neighborhood who went to our church. It was apparent how much he enjoyed this man's friendship. The man also enjoyed Terrell's company as he and his wife had no son. He would take Terrell places—like swimming and other activities. He even taught Terrell to swim.

So I decided that perhaps it would help Terrell if I would "sell out" in Cisco and move to Abilene (fifty miles away). I had a brother and sister and their families living there. In addition to their families, there were also two brothers-in-law and their families. "Surely," I thought, "this will help Terrell to have companionship that he doesn't have in Cisco."

All this I kept in my heart, and I would pray about it and God's will. I knew God would give me the answer—

He always had. I was in no hurry!

No one knew how I was praying. I didn't tell my best friend—not even my pastor.

But one Sunday night, we had a special speaker, whose sermon text was I Kings 17:10-13 regarding the widow woman and her son—relating how they were going to eat their last meager supply of meal (a handful). But the man of God came by, and she prepared a portion of the meal for him first, then for herself and her son. Then she was blessed.

A dear friend, Grace, who did not know how I was praying, came to me after dismissal of the service and said, "Bobbie, that message was for you." Of course, I too knew the sermon was for me—telling me a man of God was coming into my life soon.

Not long after this, one Sunday morning after service, Jack's cousin and other friends were talking about Jack and his lady friend having "broken up" and that they weren't going to get married. I opened my big, joking mouth and blurted, "Oh, goody, maybe *I'll* have a chance at him!"

Can you guess what Jack's cousin did? Right, again. She wrote Jack what I said. Honestly, I wasn't even thinking at that time about a man of God coming into my life. But admittedly, this triggered the thought anew.

Jack answered his cousin's letter, and asked her to ask me if he could write to me. Well, I'm not stupid! I told her "yes"!

Still, I wondered, and pondered the question: "Is this the man of God coming into my life?" I had to know again if this was really the Lord. This time I had to know through Terrell's attitude and reaction. Terrell was then sixteen years old. I had never even gone with anyone since his father died. I knew that up to that time it would have been hard for him to accept any man even going with me, or taking his daddy's place.

So my fleece and prayer to God was to let me know through Terrell's reaction to Jack's letter when it arrived. Terrell and I always ate lunch together at home. I would go by from work and pick him up at school. The mail always arrived at lunch time.

I had not told him I was expecting a letter from Jack. The day the letter arrived, he got the mail out of the box. There it was—a letter from Brother Jack Courtney, Longview, Texas. I was super-excited! But I was watching to see if *Terrell* was.

I said, "Open it! Read it to me!" Hard to believe, isn't it? But that's just what I told him! Jack wanted to come to see us. I asked, "What do you think about that?" He slid back in his chair, threw his head back with a broad grin and replied, "Get me a wet wash cloth before I faint!" He thought it would be great!

And later, when Jack had related to me how he had prayed, and the Lord had revealed His will for him through the same Scripture as He revealed it to me, we then knew beyond any shadow of doubt that we were both in the center of God's perfect will! That was, of course, a wonderful feeling beyond description!

To top it all off, on our wedding day in Cisco, God surely must have designed the weather on February 8, 1964; just for us—at least, that's how we feel. Just like spring in February—not a cloud in the sky! Literally "shirt sleeve" weather. Even the radio announcers were commenting on the *unusual* weather.

Grace called me early that morning. When I answered the phone, she started singing in her beautiful, clear voice, "Oh, what a beautiful morning, Oh what a beautiful day, I've got a wonderful feeling, everything's going my way!" To this day, that is my favorite secular song!

Another point of fact that amazes us is that Terrell was ready and willing to give up friends, to leave grandparents and his school to which he was accustomed, and to move to Longview and to a whole new life. This was a marvelous answer to prayer.

Jack and I were married by Sister Blackwell in the church. Many friends and the Longview pastor, D. L. Spears, made the trip to Cisco for the wedding, which, of course, helped make the occasion even more wonderful!

I'll never forget when we left from the wedding on our honeymoon, going to San Antonio. Terrell and a friend his age, Billy Harper, from Longview and with whom he stayed while we were gone four days, followed us in Jack's car (mine was new, so we went in it) for about two miles. Then they turned around and went back.

Upon our return to Longivew, Terrell asked Jack, "Well, Paw, you and Mom left sort of fast on your honeymoon, didn't you?"

Jack replied, "Oh no, I never went over seventy miles per hour" (the speed limit at that time). My car was new, and the speedometer had not been checked for accuracy.

Terrell said with a grin, "Something must be wrong. Billy and I clocked you at eighty-five to ninety miles per hour to keep up with you!" Sure enough, the speedometer on the new car proved to be registering fifteen to twenty miles too slow from sixty-five to seventy actual miles per hour.

Well, Jack and I had noticed how we were passing everything on the road—even motorcycles! We both wondered why everyone was driving so *slow!* But we were ignorant of the speeding. We didn't know. Not one patrol car did we see out on the highway! Does this prove that God many times takes care of idiots, drunks, and newlyweds?

Seriously, though, since those days Jack and I have walked through many hard trials and dark valleys together, and Jesus has been right there with us. I have never forgotten through the years how Jesus gave me not only a good husband, but a truly great man of God. He has also been a real dad for Terrell. God has graced our lives with a lovely grandchild, Devin Mayhall, who is twelve years old. We have seen Devin receive the Holy Ghost and be baptized in Jesus' name. He lives only fifty miles away, and we are privileged that he is with us every weekend.

Jack writes a beautiful poem for my birthday (October 12th) every year, which I treasure above all other birthday gifts. As of 1984, I have twenty-one poems. In closing, I would like to share with you one of my favorites: "Ocean Of Love."

Ocean Of Love
(October 12, 1974)

The harbor lights began to play
Around my ship of love one day.
The luring waves were softly heard
To say, "Embark now at my word."

Enchanted now, I stepped on board,
   When two hands touched, the ship unmoored.
Then gentle breezes of adoration
   Propelled this ship of our elation.

The shallow waters we had before
   Gave place at once to distant shore.
Together facing yonder sea,
   A journey of joy for you and me.

Now arm in arm on starboard side
   Thru misty waves of love we glide.
We mount the watery volume steep
   Beholding wonders of the deep.

So, ocean deep and ocean wide,
   To fathom our love, you've nobly tried.
Your depth and width are surely a symbol,
   But measure our love? You'd only fill a thimble.

So volume of love o'erflowing the sea,
   Sailing together, just you and me.
We'll face the miles, we'll love the more,
   Together, we'll reach the other shore.

Honeymooning in San Antonio (Alamo in background.)

Leaving for home after honeymoon.

First and only home of Bobbie and Jack Courtney in Longview, Texas.

Happiness is. . .

. . .the thump-thump of crutches

By Mary Dean

"I fell in love with you when you were fourteen years old," my husband still tells me. We grew up in the same small community of Ash Switch, rode the same school bus, went to the same Baptist church, and walked the same country roads. I simply have no recollection of him until we were teenagers.

I was enjoying the companionship of both sexes, with much gusto a little in love with everyone, but too serious to be serious about anyone. In order to compensate for freckles, and being slightly overweight, I was a daredevil, a cutup, and full of vim, vigor, and vitality. Also, I had a host of friends.

All of the young people of the community were church goers; I hasten to add that very few of us were religious. The church was a place to meet one's friends. However, we all were eventually convicted, joined the church, and were baptized. I do not say that it was not genuine repentance, but without the Holy Ghost in our lives, we were the same as before, and continued in our same routine. I would like to add at this point that quite a few of those young people, over the years, received the Holy Ghost and were baptized in Jesus' name.

Our social life consisted of church, weiner roasts, and just gathering at someone's house for games. One of our favorite games was "Penny goes walking." A boy dropped a penny into the cupped hand of one of the boys and a girl dropped a penny into the hand of one of the girls. The boy and girl who got the pennies had to go walking together. If a person got matched up with somone he or she didn't like too well, they made the walk a short one. If a person got someone he or she liked, it was a while before they got back.

It was on one of these long walks that I received my first kiss from my husband-to-be. I was young and inexperienced, but we both remember the time and place. At that time it made no great impact on my life (nor his either, no doubt).

The next year or so our relationship was more or less a flirtation. Bill was so much fun to be with! He had big brown eyes, black hair, and was a little over six feet tall. He was also four years older than I. Now and then, in a crowd, I would glance up and catch him looking at me in a special way. I enjoyed the attention and felt very flattered, but my heart was tuned in to another wave length at the time.

To be truthful, I was more interested in his best friend. He was a real Romeo. He could play the guitar, croon love songs, and was a neat dresser. However, he had gone with most of the girls in the community, and he wasn't too popular with the parents.

One night as he was walking me home, he said, "Mary, you're really too good for me. Why don't you go with Bill? He's a great guy and he likes you."

"If you don't want to go with me, that's okay, but you don't have to find a boyfriend for me!" I was quick to retort.

In the meantime, Bill didn't seem to be losing any sleep over me. Each time I saw him with someone else, I was overwhelmed with jealousy. I definitely didn't want anyone else to get him!

The Christmas just before my sixteenth birthday, I received gifts from four different boys at the community Christmas tree. My gift from Bill was a box of chocolate covered cherries with a dollar bill stuck under the cellophane wrap. Now in those days, a box of chocolates was a nice gift, and along with the dollar, it made quite an impression. However, the battle wasn't won yet. This particular date was Christmas Eve, 1941.

Just seventeen days earlier, I had written in my diary, *"The U.S. declared war on Japan today."* I can remember the President's speech, and wondered how it would affect our young lives. Although I couldn't really comprehend what was ahead, I knew there would be some dramatic changes in our community. Several of the boys were just the right age to enlist at the time. Bill was one of them. One by one they began to answer the call of their country.

Bill enlisted in June of 1942 and was to leave on the twenty-second. By this time, he had confessed his love for me, but I still was not sure. I knew I had a feeling for him, but I just was not sure it was the real thing.

The night before his departure, several of our friends met at one of my girlfriends' house for a little farewell get-together. Afterward, he walked me home. It was a long walk down a country road, but it ended too soon. We talked of many things. Once again he said, "I love you. Please say you'll be my girl, and wait for me until this war is over."

I was only sixteen at the time and wasn't sure I should make a commitment of this kind. I just said, "Give me a little time. . .I'll let you know."

He told me he'd write as soon as he could, and I promised I'd write him, too. He took me in his arms under a big oak tree. The moon made lacy images of the leaves overhead. Somewhere a whippoorwill sang in the night. As he kissed me goodbye, my heart was heavy. I wondered how long it would be before I looked in those big brown eyes again, and felt the touch of his hand in mine. Little did I know that his goodbye kiss would be the last for sixteen long months.

In a few days, his card came. He was in a reception center, where he had been issued GI clothing, gotten his shots, had all his hair clipped off, and was given orders to send all his civilian clothing, and personal items back home. I wrote back, *"Things are sure dull around here now. I sure do miss you."*

"I'll never forget my last night at home," he said in his next letter. *"It was the most enjoyable time I've ever*

spent with any girl. There was only one thing wrong, the promise you wouldn't make. That's why I hate to be away. You might miss me now, but you'll probably forget me before long. I will always feel the same about you, no matter what you do."

He was sent from Camp Walters to Camp Roberts, California, where he began his training. In his letters, he told of all-night hikes and complained of the heat. He always told me of his love, and that he'd always be true to me. However, he wrote: *"I want you to enjoy yourself. Go out with the boys if you like. As for me, I don't want anyone but you."*

I missed him terribly and anxiously awaited the arrival of the mail every day. *"I still can't figure you out,"* he wrote. *"You say you think of me all the time, and you're always wishing I were there. Why would you be this way if you didn't love me?"* And I began to ask myself the same question!

I had experienced the trauma of a broken home, and wanted none of this for my life. Neither did I want to make promises that I couldn't keep, therefore the caution and reluctance.

Eventually, the matter was settled in my mind. I wished that I could look in his eyes when I finally said "I love you," but I had to relay the message on paper. I promised him that I would wait for him, and I would be true to him. I'm sure he probably already knew it in his heart, but he was overjoyed that I had finally admitted it. Other boys had lost their attraction for me, and I would have to be content with a three-year courtship by mail.

On October 15 he wrote that he had passed all tests to qualify for the paratroopers. *"I'm so glad,"* he said. *"I think they are the best and the bravest fighters in the world."* He was shipped to Ft. Benning, Georgia, to begin the rigorous training that paratroopers have to go through before they get their wings.

Meanwhile, I was back in school. It was my senior year and an exciting time for me. I worked in a government job that opened up at school, and made spending money and enough to pay for all my senior expenses. Also, I had to have plenty of stamps and stationery, so I could keep my sweetheart informed of all the happenings at home.

He wrote regularly. *"After I have made five jumps,"* he said, *"I will find out if I qualify to be a paratrooper. If I do, I will get a leave, and I hope to come home and hold you in my arms again."*

He was thrilled with his first jump. *"Do you know, I could hardly believe it myself. When I got on the ground and looked up, I said to myself, 'I just wonder how you managed to do it.'"*

He did get through the tough training with flying colors, and got his coveted paratrooper wings on November 11, 1942. However, the leave we had both wanted so badly was not to be. Uncle Sam had a right to break promises if and when he chose. Instead, by Christmas, Bill had been shipped out of the country, and he wasn't allowed to tell where he was going. We did not learn until much later that he was in Panama.

He would write long letters reminiscing about the good times we had together when he was at home. *"I really didn't realize what great days those were, when we were walking together, and holding hands, just like we knew what love was all about."*

Then he'd talk about the times when he was so jealous and we'd quarrel. *"I really don't see how anyone could have gotten along with me,"* he said, *"but somehow, you did a good job of convincing me that you were the kind of girl I could never forget."*

Time passed swiftly, and before I knew it, graduation was only a month away. I received a letter from my paratrooper written on May 4. *"I've been wondering what to give you for graduation. I was thinking of sending you an engagement ring, but didn't know what you thought about it. What size do you need, Darling? It might not get there for graduation but that wouldn't matter would it?"*

What did I think about it? I was almost beside myself, although I would have liked for him to be there to place it on my finger. Sure enough, it did arrive before graduation, and I'm sure that the joy of receiving my diploma was secondary to the gleam on my finger!

Soon after graduation, I went to work in the drug store in town. Bill's sister and I rented a room together in walking distance of our jobs. I worked different shifts, so I was at home one day about noon when she called and asked me if I had my clothes on. I assured her that I did and she said, "Just wanted to know as someone is on the way to see you!"

I didn't think too much about it, so I lay back down on the bed and began reading. Presently there was a knock and the door opened. There stood my honey, looking like a million dollars in his tailored uniform, his spit shined boots, and a big smile from ear to ear! When I finally regained my voice, I squealed "Darling!" and jumped right off the bed into his outstretched arms. We had dreamed of this time for so long, and here he was in flesh and blood, and we were so in love!

The two weeks passed, oh, so swiftly. We had so much catching up to do and such a short time to do it. We talked of getting married, but he said, "No, I might get killed and you're too young to be a widow."

So once again the time came to say farewell. It was so much harder this time. The future was very uncertain, and we both knew what we wanted—a life together with no interruptions. We kissed goodbye and he said, "Go and don't look back." When I returned to my room, the tears poured forth. I cried the rest of the day and was hard to live with the rest of the week.

He had one more short leave, and then he was shipped overseas to the European theatre. He made his first combat jump in France and the jump was fine, but he was wounded later in the day, in the hip and leg. He was carried to a barn where he lay for several days before the medics could get to him. By the time he got to a hospital in Italy, infection had already spread to his stomach. He came so near death that the curtain was pulled around his bed and the chaplain came to see him. But the angel of the Lord came also and delivered him from the jaws of death!

When he regained his strength, he wrote, *"Just to let you know I'm getting well fast, and expect to be walking soon, and also that I love you as much as a person could love anyone. I don't think it will be too long until I'm back with the rest of the guys."*

That fall, I talked my dad into letting me go to Dallas and get a job. All of my friends had already left, either to the service or to jobs out of town. One of my girlfriends was in Dallas already and said we could get an apartment together. I was glad to get away, as there were too many memories of happier days at home. I landed a job the first day at Sears Roebuck in the mail order department.

Bill left the hospital and went back to the front lines of battle. In every letter he talked of his longing to come home. Once he said, *"If it weren't for this war, I'd probably be home now with a couple of kids on my knee."*

In January of 1945, he was wounded again in the Battle of the Bulge. At this particular time, a German tank had a bunch of men penned down and was going down the line mowing them down. If they got up and ran, they were shot; if they just lay where they were, they were shot. So the only alternative was prayer. They were lying behind fence posts for a little protection. The gunner was going right down that row of posts. Somebody's husband died, then somebody's dad, and someone's son. As the gunner came on down the line toward Bill, he laid his head down in the snow and prayed, "Lord, if you'll just let me live, I'll do anything you want me to do."

The next shot was supposed to be his. Miraculously, and for no apparent reason, the tank raised its gun, cranked up, and left! He had been wounded, slightly, in the arm, but he lay in the snow until the darkness allowed his escape. This was one time he didn't mind the wound too much, as it got him out of the battle for awhile.

From the hospital he wrote: *"I expect to go back to the outfit about the 17th. I don't know how I'll come out this time, but I'm pretty sure, one of these days it will be finished for me."*

Talk like this really disturbed me, as he was usually more optimistic. I continued to pray in my own way, and tried to encourage him as much as I could in my letters, but he wasn't getting his mail regularly then. At this time I also had a brother in the Europe war, and I prayed that God would be merciful and bring them back to us. This was a time of stress and apprehension for America. Not many families went untouched by the horrors of war. Telegrams were being sent by the government to families every day relaying the message that some loved one had been killed or wounded.

Once more, Bill was sent back to the front. His unit had been completely wiped out and the guys he was with were all strangers. His morale was at a low ebb, but he wanted to live, so he did whatever was needful to stay alive. He was wounded again, the last day of the war in Europe. This time he was shot in the heel by a sniper, and the bullet exploded in his foot. The bone was shattered, so there would be no more combat for him.

He was put on a hospital ship and landed in Charleston, South Carolina, on June 6, 1945. He wrote from there: *"I expect to be coming to a hospital in Texas by the time you get this. However, I must go where they can treat my foot. Haven't heard from you since I left Germany. Hope you send a telegram tonight."* I did. . .and gave him a telephone number to call collect.

At this time, I was living in a boarding house for girls, and the word had gotten around that he was supposed to call. When my call finally came through, everyone came running. I was so excited that my heart was going haywire! The girls were all standing around trying to share my excitement and happiness. Most of them were either engaged or married to a soldier.

After we had talked awhile, he asked me, "Do you still want to marry me?"

"Why do you think I've been waiting all these years?" I answered.

"Even if I'm crippled?"

"Who cares about that?" I said. Needless to say, I didn't sleep much that night.

He didn't get sent to Texas, but to a hospital in Okmulgee, Oklahoma. He wrote from there. *"As soon as I get my pay straightened out, I'm gonna call you and tell you to come on up."*

In the meantime, I made plans to go see him on a weekend. His sister and another friend were going also. When he got my letter saying I was coming, he called, "I can't stand for you to come and leave me again. Why don't we just get married when you come?"

Well, I was all for that! But it didn't give me much time to give notice on my job, shop for a trousseau, and take care of other business there. However, I had waited too long for this event to be deterred by trivialities, so I said, "Okay!" and hung up with my mind in a whirl.

I was on a bus headed for Okmulgee a few short days later, and my long-awaited reunion with my sweetheart. I had not seen him in eighteen months, but hadn't given a thought about whether he had changed, or what the war had done to him. My only concern at the moment was getting to him and seeing for myself that he had really gotten back home alive and safe. The ride was a long one, but I was too excited to read or sleep. . .and I knew that somewhere up ahead somebody else was just as excited and losing some sleep, too!

He had rented a room and given me instructions about the location, asking me to go there as soon as I arrived. Shortly after I arrived, he called. "Don't come out of that room when I come," he cautioned. He was to catch a bus from the hospital after lunch, and all of the boys wanted to witness the great "reunion." I arranged my hair, put on my prettiest dress. . .and waited.

Presently I heard the sound of crutches bump-bumping against the floor outside. My heart was pounding with anticipation, but I waited for his knock. When it came, I opened the door and he slipped inside and closed it before we reached for each other. The joy of that meeting could never be expressed in words. The memory of it still excites me! We were together again and this time it was for always!

"You looked so grown-up," he said later. Except for the cast and crutches, he was the same. He could stand some meat on his bones, but I would see to that later.

We were married that evening at eight o'clock by a Presbyterian minister whom we had never seen before and haven't seen since. It was a beautiful ceremony, and at last our dreams had come true! I was now Mrs. William H. Dean. So long I had coveted that title—and I would bear it proudly.

We had a four-month honeymoon before he was discharged with a medical disability. He was at the hospital during the day, but he was free to come home at night. If something came up that he couldn't come home, I caught a bus and went to see him. We didn't have a care. It didn't cross our minds about how we'd make a living after his discharge. We were so happy just to be together that nothing else mattered. No clouds dimmed our horizon during that time. We set out to catch up on the time we had lost and we did a good job!

When he was discharged, we moved back to our

hometown and bought a small house and ten acres of land for $750. This money he had saved while he was in the service. It wasn't a mansion, but we were so proud of our home and our second-hand furniture. We still call it our honeymoon house.

When we finally settled in and got back to normal, we started going to the church we had gone to before we left. Bill had not forgotten what he had promised the Lord on that cold January day. This was all he knew to do, until the Lord directed him otherwise.

Our first son was born in December of 1946. We were very happy! A boy was just what Bill wanted, and he was right there holding my hand through it all.

One of the young men in the community had received the Holy Ghost while in the service. When Bill heard of it, he made a special trip to his house to ask him more about it. He wasn't home, but his mom told Bill where he went to church. We made plans to go the following Sunday. If there was something missing in our lives, we wanted to find out what it was.

Well, it was quite an experience! We had never seen such carrying-on in church, and didn't go back for a while. However, the next time we went Bill got up during testimony service and said, "I don't have this Holy Ghost, and I would like to have it," and marched right down to the altar. We both eventually received this great experience. A few months later, the Lord sent Brother Lonnie Hosch to unveil the truth of baptism in Jesus' name to us, and we consecrated our lives to the Lord.

When Bill was thirty-six years old, the Lord called him into the ministry. We had four boys and another one on the way when we took our first church. We left a nice home and a good paying job and went to a small home missions work, but we never lacked for necessities.

Today, we have a good church in Killeen, Texas, a military town. For the past sixteen years, we have ministered to soldiers and their families. We feel they are a great people to work with, and many have served their time in service and remained to help us. We can speak their language and know their problems.

Our five sons are all licensed ministers, serving in different capacities all over the country. We dedicated them all to the Lord when they were small, so we hestiate to complain about hardly ever seeing them or our ten grandchildren.

Meanwhile, our honeymoon continues. If the Lord allows us to live until June 30 of 1985, we will celebrate our fortieth anniversary. We are more in love than ever. The blessings of the Lord have enriched our lives, and we are very thankful!

Billy and Mary Dean, July, 1945.

The Dean Family, 1982.

Happiness is. . .

...a pair of
long eyelashes

By Roffie Ensey

There they lay in the corner of the drawer, exactly where I had placed them several years ago.

They were in a brown envelope, neatly packaged. Some were addressed to Rev. Jerry Ensey and some were addressed to Miss Roffie Oliver. As I took them out and began to read the love letters, my mind was flooded with memories of years gone by. I remembered the stories told to me about Jerry's childhood, and marveled at the hand of God in both our lives.

It happened like this.
On August 28, 1938, in a little log cabin near Hugo,

Oklahoma, a son was born to the Ensey family. Destiny dictated that he would be deeply involved in the work of God.

The Ensey family lived in Hugo until Jerry was about three years old. At this time they moved to Odell, a small town in the northwest Texas "dustbowl." In 1947, the Great Depression and the war years behind, they moved to Vernon, Texas, which became home until Jerry was grown.

Jerry was raised in a very close family. He, along with his brother and sister, may not have always had everything they wanted materially, but they always knew they were loved. I have heard them tell many times how their mother made all their clothes, cut the boys' hair until they were teenagers, cooked good meals for them and always kept everything spotlessly clean. The children attended Baptist churches in Vernon and Odell, but Bible study and the family altar were not a part of their family life.

When Jerry was attending Vernon High School, he signed up for the Distributive Education Program and got a job at a factory where Boy Scout trousers were made.

On his first day at work, he was assigned to work in the department where there was a young lady who attended the United Pentecostal Church. He noticed there was something different about her. She wore no make-up, her hair was uncut, and her attitude distinguished her from the others. He greatly admired her, but because of peer pressure, he chided her along with the rest.

One day she began to talk with him about visiting her church. He wasn't interested. But then a friend said, "Yes, let's go with her." (The friend was interested in the girl and not in church.)

The first service Jerry attended was a youth rally where Brother W. C. Parkey was the speaker. He and his friend laughed at the way these strange people worshiped, but the music and the singing were delightfully different.

Deciding to try another service, they ventured to a tent revival. The minister preached about Sodom and Gomorrah; when these names were first mentioned, Jerry thought the minister was talking about husband and wife! By the time the message was finished, however, he knew he had some decisions to make. He could almost feel the heat!

A few days later, on August 7, 1955, he attended the church in Vernon and went to the altar. After a time of repenting, he went home, grabbed a change of clothes, and returned to be baptized in a stock pond. The next night, he received the gift of the Holy Ghost. Brother and Sister E. L. Holley were among those praying with him that night.

As Jerry grew in the Lord, he felt a call to preach, and on January 27, 1956, he preached his first sermon. The following November he received his local license with the United Pentecostal Church. He held his first revival in Iowa Park, Texas, in April of 1957. On June 1, 1957, he and another young minister quit their jobs to give their full time to evangelistic work. That was the year of the first youth camp in Texas, and so they came to Lufkin to attend.

My early life was quite different. I was born on October 20, 1941. There was already a little boy in the family, and later four more boys and another girl would come along. My parents named me after my great-aunt Roffie.

We were living in Hempstead, Texas, at that time. Short-ly thereafter, we moved to Silsbee, where we lived until I married.

Our family was also a very close-knit family. There was always plenty of love to go around, even with seven children. Creature comforts were not always available, but the needs were met.

The main thing I remember about my early childhood was that God always came first in our family. We attend-ed the First United Pentecostal Church in Silsbee, where both Mother and Daddy taught Sunday school classes. When any of us were sick, the first thing to do was to call our pastor for prayer! Most Sundays there was company over at our house. Mother was an excellent cook and everyone always had a good time.

The church in Silsbee had a large youth group and was very pleased when the Texas District decided to have an annual youth camp. At the age of 16, I attended this first Youth Camp in 1957.

Sister Bessie Pugh was the registrar. When I came to register, there was a surprised look on her face. Sister Pugh explained that look when she said, "You're Roffie? Oh, with that name, I have put you in the boy's dorm!" Needless to say, other arrangements were made!

At this youth camp, two very important things hap-pened in my life. I received the gift of the Holy Ghost, and I met my husband. Of course, I had no idea at the time that Jerry Ensey would someday be my husband. I had seen him around camp all week. He was that nice look-ing young evangelist with the big brown eyes and the long eyelashes.

On the last day of camp before everyone left, there

were a lot of pictures being taken. I finally had an opportunity to meet Jerry and happened to be standing talking
with him when a young lady came by and wanted to take
our picture together. He was very much opposed to the
idea and actually refused to have his picture made with
me! My thoughts of him were not too kind at that time.
I promptly dismissed him from my mind and really never
expected to see him again.

I went home from youth camp with a zeal and desire
to work for the Lord. I was asked to play the piano for
our church services; I agreed to try, even though I had
only had a few lessons. There were many times when I
would have to stop and let the congregation sing acap-
pella until I could find my place again!

After graduating from high school, I attended a
business college and secured a job at the local bank. One
night while attending our office Christmas party, I received
a phone call. When they told me it was long distance and
a man, I didn't believe them. I was not expecting a call
from anyone, much less a man!

It was Jerry! He asked if I remembered him. Of
course, I remembered! I remembered that he had brown
eyes and long eyelashes! He asked if he could come see
me on Friday night.

In December of 1959, we had our first date. (We were
"chaperoned" by an area pastor friend and his wife.) He
took me to a fancy restaurant in Beaumont and we dined
by candlelight!

I wanted desperately to impress him in the right way.
I wanted to do everything just right, but since this was the
first time I had ever been to such a fancy place, I was quite
nervous. I had read a few love stories, and it seemed that

the man always ordered for his date, so I told Jerry to just order for me. (He was probably just as nervous as I!) All too soon the meal was over and it was time to leave. I was enjoying just being with him, but how long can you just sit in a restaurant?

When he took me home I invited him in for a while. I wanted him to meet my family. They were all impressed with my charming young evangelist! After staying for what he felt was an appropriate time, he got up to leave. I walked with him to the door and he just stood there. His long, lingering look indicated he had really enjoyed himself and hated to go. Finally, he blinked those long eyelashes at me and asked if he could come back. My heart did a flip-flop and I completely forgot that this was the same young man who would not allow his picture to be taken with me! I was smitten, and so was he! I fluttered my eyes and said, "Of course, I would like for you to come back. Anytime!"

Anytime was just a few days later. He called to say he would pick me up from work, but before he arrived, a record snow storm was underway. By the time he picked me up, several inches had fallen and the roads were treacherous. When we finally got to my house, it was so bad that he couldn't leave. Tsk! Tsk! He was *forced* to spend the night at my house!

That was the biggest snow in Silsbee in years—twelve inches! This gave him time to really get acquainted with my family. After spending the night in the same room with my five brothers, one would think he would be ready to leave as soon as possible. But to my delight, he spent the whole day with us. We played in the melting snow, took pictures, visited my aunt and uncle, and just had a good time.

On January 1, 1960, my oldest brother married my best friend. Jerry had a few free days around that time, so he came to attend the wedding with me. Then he was off to Louisiana for revivals he had scheduled.

One night before he left, we had gone somewhere and just as we were arriving back at my house, he began to talk about what it meant to be a minister's wife. He must have talked for at least ten minutes. (I later learned this was just his way.)

All the time he was talking, my mind was racing. Where was he going? What is he getting at? Is this going to be a proposal? I already knew what my answer would be if it was! My heart was in my throat when he finally put his arm around me and said three of the most beautiful words in the world—"I love you!"

This declaration was followed by the big question. When he said "Roffie, will you marry me?" I didn't have to hesitate. I already knew that he was the right one for me! My answer was yes, so before he left on January 9, we were engaged privately. He did not want anyone to know until he had time to talk with Daddy. Daddy's working schedule made it difficult to find time to talk with him.

That first night he wrote me a letter from West Monroe, Louisiana. The next night he wrote me from Minden where he was starting a revival. He said he was trying to set a good example for me to follow! On the first night of his revival, he wrote that he started to sing a chorus when he got up but couldn't remember the tune. The chorus was "Old Time Religion"! He was truly bitten by the "love bug."

Around the end of January, he was able to come back to Silsbee for a day or two. At this time we talked with my parents about getting married. Of course, they already suspected we were getting serious!

My daddy was a plumbing and electrical contractor. When Jerry sat down to ask him for his blessings, he had a little trouble getting to the reason for his visit. He began by telling him he needed to ask him something. They talked about the weather, his revivals, and anything else that came to mind. Finally he decided it was time to ask the big question, so he said: "Ahh, uhh, Brother Oliver, uhh, ahh, how's the plumbing business?"

Of course, Daddy knew what he wanted to talk with him about and it was *not* the plumbing business! He finally got it said and Mother and Daddy were both pleased. We began to plan for the wedding, which was scheduled for April 12, 1960.

It was not easy to make all the plans through letters and over the phone, but somehow we managed. As I read over the letters we wrote during this time, I noticed there was not much about wedding plans. Mostly we just talked about how much we missed each other. In one of the letters I wrote to Jerry, I told him how much the flowers were going to cost. My bouquet was only $15.00 and the total cost for all flowers was less than $60.00! (My, how times have changed!)

Since his family lived so far away, I would not have an opportunity to meet them before the wedding, so I began to correspond with his mother and sister right away. Betty was to be the matron of honor and Harold, Jerry's brother, was to be his best man. I was anxious to get acquainted with all of them, because they would be my family after the wedding. Of course, it pleased Jerry that I wanted to get to know them and whatever pleased him is what I wanted most!

Jerry was gone until about two weeks before the wedding. He arranged to preach the remainder of the time near Silsbee so he could help with the last minute details.

When we married, the financial resources were very meager. I received a refund from the IRS of $85.00 just a week before the wedding and this was my gift to Jerry. His gift to me was a beautiful watch. Our wedding day dawned bright, beautiful, clear, and sunny! Everything was just perfect.

Jerry came to the house that afternoon and we loaded the car. Everything was ready for us to leave on our honeymoon as soon as the reception was over. We were married in the church at Silsbee, with Brother Harry Morgan performing the ceremony.

After the reception, we drove to Beaumont where we had reservations for the night. When we arrived at the motel, my husband went in to register and the man told him he had already let someone else have our room because they were expecting us earlier. It took what seemed like an eternity to find a place to spend the night. We settled for a little motel so close to the Gulf of Mexico that we could almost hear the waves on the beach.

We had about two weeks before our next revival started and some very dear friends of ours let us spend the last few days of our honeymoon in their home while they were away on vacation.

This all happened twenty-five years ago. During those years God has blessed us with two fine children, a lovely daughter-in-law and three precious grandchildren. Today my heart is filled with gratitude for God and His blessings to us. Yes, He does all things well!

A lot of changes have taken place during the past years, but one thing hasn't changed—Jerry still has the ability to make my heart flutter with those long eyelashes!

Playing in the snow.

The Ensey Evangelistic Team.

Wedding Reception.

Happiness is. . .

. . .gathering water lilies

By Forrest H. and
Annie M. Ford

"*Right on time*" thought Forrest, as the bus pulled into the Overton station. Reaching for his old delapidated suitcase that had been patched with some adhesive tape and dyed with black liquid shoe polish, Forrest pulled it down from the overhead rack.

He had prayed for the Lord to make a way so that he could obey his call to the ministry and here was the answer—a bus fare ticket to a place where he had never been, to a church he had never seen, and to a minister he had never met. The letter had said, "I have heard that you are good at working with young people and we are needing a youth revival, so here is your fare to come and preach it; we will meet you at the bus station." Well, here he was. So what now? He was soon to find out!

The little station, setting in the small oilfield town, seemed anything but cheery. The only passenger emerging for this destination, he had hardly stepped from the bus when Pastor Merle Hendrickson, his wife, and two small sons moved forward to meet him.

"So this is Evangelist Forrest Ford!" exclaimed Pastor Hendrickson, extending his hand of greeting with a warm and friendly handclasp, while the family offered greetings also. "I'm Merle Hendrickson, the pastor of the Turner-town church and this is my family."

"Glad to meet you," answered the young minister, looking into the kindly face of a man who would make a great contribution to the life of one who had such a small and unknown beginning.

The pastor's wife was just as friendly, with a gentle and comforting voice. The two boys seemed overjoyed, the older asking, "Daddy, is this the young preacher you said you were sending for?"

"Thank heaven," thought the evangelist. *"At least they have been well trained."*

The old car pulled away, transporting its cargo over a rough oilfield road, and came to rest at an unpainted shack that was as neat and clean as could be on the inside.

Meanwhile, the pastor had glanced at the young minister beside him, seeing a slender and blue-eyed man with light brown hair. He carried himself erect, and the forehead of his boyish face was emphasized with a few waves in his hair which was parted and combed back. *"I wonder what kind of a preacher he will be?"* Pastor Hendrickson thought, but he was to be well pleased. This was the beginning of a new life for this young minister from which *"out of the depth"* would come love that he had never known.

"Would you like to go over to the church and look it over while Mother prepares some supper?" Pastor Hendrickson asked, upon arriving at the parsonage.

"Oh, yes, I would like that very much," answered Forrest.

Observing Forrest, the pastor wondered why he was just now beginning his ministry. He broke the silence, saying, "It's not a very beautiful building and neither do we have a large congregation, but we hope that we will have a great revival and begin to grow."

"I'm anxious to get started, though the thought scares me a bit," admitted Forrest as they walked into the building. The success story had begun.

Days passed and the services were indescribably wonderful! One day, everyone had gathered in the modest little living room to listen to a radio program sponsored by a church of like faith in Kilgore, Texas. As the program came over the air, immediately Forrest's attention was drawn to the lyric soprano voice singing in a duet, then a quartet. He strained as though trying to identify the source from which it came.

"Oh, how beautiful!" he thought. Then with intense earnestness, he looked at the pastor and exclaimed, "I sure would like to meet the young lady who is singing the soprano!"

"You will," answered Pastor Hendrickson, "this very afternoon. She will be here for the youth rally."

"Really! Oh, good!" he answered. Then, realizing that he had shown his inner feelings, he blushed. The wise pastor only smiled, and then said, "She is a very beautiful Christian young lady."

Would rally time never come? Impatient? Yes! But the time did come and the evangelist stationed himself at the door with the pastor to welcome the guests. Each time the door opened, the evangelist's heart seemed to skip several beats, thinking the next one to enter would be the young lady. This day was never to be forgotten!

The young Christian lady Forrest was so eager to meet had been saved in a revival in Kilgore under the ministry of Evangelist Taylor F. Ford (no relation). She had received the Holy Spirit and was baptized in Jesus' name at the age of eleven and was now a grown teenager singing solos and participating in a church duet, trio, and quartet, as well as the choir. The Lord had blessed her with the beautifully pleasing voice which attracted the attention of the young minister named Forrest Ford, who had been filled with the Spirit of the Lord and baptized in His name at the age of nineteen. This girl, Annie Merle Camp, had heard her Grandmother Camp pray many times for the Lord to give her, as well as her younger sister, a good Christian companion. Her parents were exemplary Christians also.

Annie Merle was very excited and looked forward to attending the youth rally at Turnertown! To her, this was always a great time of worship and fellowship. It was also somewhere to go. At rallies young people had a chance to meet others. Little did she realize that today she would meet a young man that would, in time to come, change her whole life!

"Perhaps she would never be interested in me" was Forrest's first thought. How wrong he was!

Finally, after anxious moments and new acquaintances, the door of the church opened and in stepped his "Cinderella." *"What beauty!"* he thought, *"And a Christian."* Her complexion was a natural life-pink with no make-up, and her hair as dark as a raven's with a touch of auburn in it, reflecting the light overhead. Her eyes were a deep brown and so beautiful! They seemed like a fountain covered by a delicate mist, but shining with youth and vigor. Everything about her fulfilled the young evangelist's dream.

He was brought off his "cloud nine" by the pastor's voice saying, "Brother Forrest, I want you to meet Sister Annie Merle Camp from Kilgore, and Sister Annie Merle, this is our evangelist, Brother Forrest Ford." With a lump in his throat, Forrest extended his hand and clasped hers. That did it! He did not want to let go. He again thought within himself, *"She will never be interested in me!"* Little did he know she was thinking the same thoughts about him.

During the rally it was announced that there would be a conference, known as the South Central Council, held in Kilgore that fall. *"Oh, great! I'll get to see her again!"* Forrest's heart began to pound. (This was the conference in which Oneness Jesus Name Sunday school literature was initiated by Reverend T. F. Ford. In fact, several things began here!)

At the conference she was with her parents, who were fine people. When the evangelist tried to attract her attention, she returned a beautiful, yet bashful smile. Finally it happened! They were together! He did not have a car of his own to offer her a ride, but he searched for an excuse to get away from the crowd with her. Remembering that he had a letter that needed mailing, he asked her if she would like to ride with him to the post office and back. She graciously accepted, so he made his way to Sister Hendrickson and asked if he could use the car to go mail a letter.

"Who is going with you?" she inquired.

"Sister Annie Merle is going to ride up and back with me."

"Sure, you may go," she replied, "but I'll have to go along and do the driving."

Bang! went his plans! Nevertheless, they did go—and they got the chance to exchange addresses. What courting! Teachings were strict in those days; the youth were taught to be very careful, shun the appearance of evil, keep themselves from all reproach, and to conduct themselves always as Christians. With no rebellion in their hearts, they obeyed.

Evangelist Ford made his plans to sit by Annie Merle in the Kilgore Convention services at night, but that plan was interrupted. A young man by the name of Corlis Dees came early enough to take his place and push Annie Merle down to the next person, leaving no room beside her for the preacher! All of this brought humorous memories when they met together in later years.

When the Council came to a close and the goodbyes were said, each was to write to the other, but this did not happen. In September of 1937, they met again in Tulsa, Oklahoma, at the National Conference of the Pentecostal Assemblies of Jesus Christ.

Forrest had been tutored under Pastor J. E. Dillon and his good wife Letha, for whom he had the highest respect. Pastor V. A. Guidroz, who pastored the church in Cleveland, Texas, where Forrest had prayed through, baptized him in Jesus' name. Brother Guidroz was greatly respected. (He seemed to have the eye of an eagle!) His wisdom in counseling was superb. With these two ministers guiding him, Forrest knew that he must be careful in courting girls. Their advice had been, "You'll meet pretty girls in every church you go to. You can drop one for the next. If you do, they may backslide; then pastors will not want you to preach for them." This advice is still true today.

There were other wise men that he listened to, including O. F. Fauss, Donald Berry, C. P. Williams, Claude Kilgore, and W. T. Witherspoon.

During the General Conference in Tulsa, after the day services were over, Forrest and Annie Merle could be seen strolling along the banks of the Arkansas River hand in hand. Heaven holds all their secrets that none will ever know until we get there, but they fell deeply in love. This is yet another time when from *"out of the depth"* came love, and it was sanctioned in heaven.

After parting in Tulsa, Forrest left for Iowa to preach for Brother D. D. Dainty; he travelled from there to St. Paul, Minnesota, to attend Apostolic Bible Institute. This was another great change in the life of this young minister, sacrificing to leave his beloved behind in Texas. Although the college was wonderful, the months seemed to drag by. But the President, Brother S. G. Norris, his wife, the faculty, students, and church were so kind and thoughtful that Forrest will always appreciate them for their teaching and guidance. The Lord knew the desire of the young minister's heart and was preparing him for a great work in the future.

Correspondence between Texas and Minnesota was very regular. The ministry was discussed; the theme of the letters was working together for the Lord. Finally, he became so lonesome to see his hope-to-be bride that space here would not permit a revelation of the contents of all those love letters!

Coming in from work one night, Forrest stopped by the auditorium to pray. The snow was deep and the weather miserably cold, making him more lonesome for the sunny south. . .and for Annie Merle! He became broken in spirit under his burden, seeking the will of God. As he prayed, someone stole in very quietly.

When his praying ceased, Pastor S. G. Norris' voice spoke softly, "Brother Ford, are you having some difficulty?"

Feeling relieved, he began to unburden his heart to Pastor Norris.

"Have you ever worn glasses?" Pastor Norris asked.

"Yes, sir."

"Then I want you to get you some more."

"But I can't. I don't have money to pay my room and board and buy glasses!"

"You don't owe any room and board until you get glasses. I'll take care of all that."

Forrest learned that Pastor Norris loved and cared for his students.

At last the day came for the old train to pull out of the depot, heading south with Evangelist Forrest Ford on board. The metal wheels, clicking on the tracks, seemed to hum a love song as the train moved along on its way to Kilgore, Texas. As he rode, Forrest tried to memorize phrases to use when he proposed to Annie Merle. (He was wasting his time, as the phrases were not to work as he supposed.) He realized that he did not have any worldly goods to offer Annie Merle and did not know what the future held. But faith—what little he knew about it—would take care of everything! Pastor Norris had taught to ask in Jesus' name, believe, and receive. Well, that should do the job!

At the state line, the Texas map sign caught Forrest's attention. *"I love Texas country!"* he thought, relaxing somewhat and watching the picturesque panorama from the train window. *"It looks like a series of patchwork quilts. . .so rich and colorful, especially in the springtime. There's beautiful farmland, rolling hills, and breathtaking cities. Of all states, I love Texas best. This is my home, my native state. . .I was born here and so was Annie Merle."*

Annie Merle was intently watching the clock. It would soon be time to meet the train that would bring her "prince" to her! *"But what if he were not on it? He's just got to be!"* she reassured herself. Her mother drove her to the station to meet him.

Forrest looked out the window. The sign said "Longview, Texas." The next town was Kilgore, his destination, which was only twelve miles farther. Excitedly, he collected his belongings. *"Will she be there? She said she would, so why should I worry so?"* He must straighten his tie, brush his teeth, and comb his hair. He had to hurry!

The train screeched to a halt; passengers began to disembark. Annie Merle watched anxiously. *"Will he never get off?"* Then, there he stood on the steps, looking toward them! He was even more handsome than she had remembered. She moved toward him, wanting to fall into his arms, but restrained herself from doing so and only shook his hand. She had been taught that embracing and touching were to be kept for marriage. Holy matrimony in the Lord would provide for all the beauties of love. True love was forever!

The Kilgore church was in revival, so to church they went. . .the whole family in one car. After the church service and back home, they strolled around the house, holding hands and smelling the perfumed odor of the honeysuckles.

Again, Corlis Dees was present and the idea of prayer moved on him and to the wagon bed he went. (It was parked under a lean-to attached to the garage.) From there, he could both "watch and pray." Each time the young couple rounded the corner, they could see his head raise up and peep at them. It seemed that eyes were everywhere! To this day, they still laugh together about this.

As they strolled in the early evening hours, it seemed that the whole world was aglow with the light of glittering stars and a radiant Texas moon. They thanked the Lord, who in His wonder, brought them together.

"He's wonderful, and so are you, my dear," said Forrest, as they walked side by side. "He has given me far more than I deserved when he gave me you."

"That's what *I* was just going to say," she answered with a smile. "I was going to say that He gave *me* much more than I deserved. He gave you to me when I thought that it could never happen. Aren't we doubting many times, when we know that the Lord answers prayer?"

"We need never doubt Him again, darling," he answered softly. "We will always be safe in Him."

"I know now that I can fully trust Him with my whole life," she said and felt his hand close tightly over hers. "We know who holds the future and He holds our hands."

Herman Campbell, who was an evangelist and good friend, came to the revival and invited Forrest to go home with him for a day or two. "Have you asked Annie Merle to marry you?" he asked Forrest pointedly.

"No, not yet."

"Really, why?" inquired Herman. "You must be afraid to ask her. . .afraid she might refuse you. Tell you what, *I'll* ask her *for* you."

"No, you won't!" a startled Forrest immediately answered. "I'll ask for myself, Herman Campbell! I am not a Captain John Smith!"

"I'm sorry," Herman apologized. "I meant no harm." And the two shook hands understandingly.

A day or so later, the young couple sat in the porch swing, talking. Each expected the other, just any minute, to mention marriage. Earlier, Forrest had gone off alone to a place of prayer and poured his heart out to God. He had both fasted and prayed, seeking God's proper timing. Now, he felt the assurance that this would be the time to propose to her. With a sigh, he turned and asked, "Will you marry me? I need you for my wife."

She looked at him tenderly, then softly answered, "But I can only cook cornbread and cake."

Quickly (lest she should change the subject), he assured, "But I can cook and I will teach you how!"

She placed her hand in his and lovingly answered, "If I am the girl for you, then you are the boy for me." In a split second, the whole world seemed to burst into glorious light!

They made their proclamation to the family and, within a few hours, were on their way to secure the marriage license.

As soon as they returned to the house, he caught her in his arms, buried his face in her hair. "I love you, darling, more than I do my own life!" He kissed her tenderly.

"I love you, too." He felt her soft arms tighten around his neck. *"This is heaven! In a few hours, we will be husband and wife!"*

She fell into his arms, saying nothing, only nestling against him in absolute bliss. Then he held her away from him for a moment and looked deeply into her eyes, whispering, "Annie Merle, darling! I am the happiest and most fortunate man in this world to find a Christian girl as beautiful as you are to be my companion for life."

Raising her head, their eyes met and she knew, with a sudden leaping in her heart, that the feeling was mutual—and that they were destined to have many happy years together. There would be no living in a fool's paradise. Forrest had dreamed of this moment months ago. . .the moment he would hold her in his arms and tell her how very much he loved her.

On Sunday, April 3, 1938, there was to be a Sunday school rally in the morning and a youth rally in the afternoon, with a great fellowship lunch in between. This was the time that Forrest and Annie Merle selected for their wedding!

At high noon, Mrs. L. O. Robinson, the church pianist, began playing the wedding march. The auditorium was filled with flowers, people, and gifts. . .but most of all, with the presence of the Lord. Standing before the altar, they were united in marriage by Pastor Taylor F. Ford. When

he pronounced them husband and wife, Forrest and Annie Merle fully realized that God had answered their prayers.
Hand in hand they faced the future together to work for
the Lord.

Following the wedding and gift presentation, it was
proclaimed to the whole congregation that the church dinner would be their wedding dinner and all were invited to
eat. What a feast! Everyone had a wonderful time—
especially Forrest's best man, Evangelist Herman Campbell and Annie Merle's maid of honor, Evie Lee Gary.

As badly as the newlyweds wanted to be alone, they
stayed for the youth rally. Then a couple in the church,
dear family friends, took them for a joy ride and treat. (They
still laugh themselves into tears when they think of it now.)
And that night, they attended the church service as
Evangelist and Mrs. Forrest H. Ford.

A honeymoon was out of the question; they had no
money or car. But that came years later when their church
sent them on an expense-paid trip to Hawaii, with accom-
modations in the best of hotels, and money to enjoy
themselves "first class." God certainly made it all up to
them, besides giving their church one of the greatest revivals it ever had! Ask them. They'll tell you quickly that
you never lose by obeying the Lord without complaining.

On Tuesday after the wedding, a black car drove into
the driveway. Pastor John Esker Dillon and wife had sent
Uncle John Die, an older minister, to provide transportation for the newlyweds to Batson, Texas, where they were
to conduct their first revival.

They had been in Batson only a short time when
Pastor Dillon told them that he had a Model A Ford, but
no tires for it. He had ordered some from Speigel's, and

when they came in, he said, Forrest and Annie Merle could use the vehicle. How thrilled they were! It seemed an eternity before the order came, but at length the car was ready to go. So off they went on a joy ride with the chance to be alone, driving to Daisetta, about ten miles away.

On the way back, Annie Merle saw some water lilies blooming in the roadside ditch and exclaimed, "Oh, I'd just *love* to have some of those!" So Forrest stopped the car and pulled up a couple of the whole plants. When they reached the Dillons, he filled a tub with water and put the plants into it.

Upon seeing the lilies and learning what they had done, Letha Dillon said very seriously, "You should have never done that! It is against the law and the police may drive up any time now and you will have to pay a big fine or go to jail."

It scared the two so badly that they feared that every car they heard was the police. They had a big laugh when they learned that she was only kidding them.

From here, they went to Beaumont, Texas, to assist Pastor John Die of Northend Pentecostal Church, eventually taking a position with the South Central Council Publishing House. Forrest wrote Sunday school literature, edited a religious paper and printing, published a funeral and wedding manual, wrote sermon outlines, and a child's Bible story book. He also served as bookkeeper, linotype operator, and kept apartments rented in the upstairs part of the building.

Their first pastorate was at Turnertown, the place where they first met at the youth rally! In the same rundown oilfield house where he lived with the Hendricksons a few years before, they set up housekeeping. Here God blessed them; the old church was revived, surging from seventeen to ninety-seven in three months.

Here, they unselfishly took a young evangelist and his wife who had no place to go and had been sleeping in their old car. Little did they know what they let themselves in for! Delivery time came for the expectant mother. What on earth were they to do? They had no money, so going to a hospital was out.

The doctor came, and began issuing orders. "I don't have a nurse with me, so you'll have to assist me."

"Oh, God, help us," prayed Forrest, and Annie Merle looked as if she were going to faint. What an experience for a young couple who had no children of their own and knew not what to expect! They learned that day that the ministry entails many strange demands, but a healthy baby boy brought happy smiles.

After resigning the Turnertown church, they evangelized again, preaching revivals and then established a church in Jacksonville, Texas, where there had not been a Pentecostal church. They only had three people when they started the revival. The family of Jerry Ward, now pastoring in Houston, was among the first to come into the church. Today, there is a beautiful church in Jacksonville.

They returned to Kilgore for the birth of their first child, a beautiful girl with her mother's features. Dorothy Ann was their pride and joy. The whole church loved her and helped to "spoil" her. She, her husband (Larry Wiggins, originally from Pastor Dillon's church), and son, Forrest David Wiggins, are in Faith Tabernacle U.P.C. in Humble, pastored by her father.

From Kilgore, the path of service led to South Bend,

Indiana, where they assisted Pastor Rowe. Here Forrest served as Junior Elder, Sunday school teacher, Youth Director, as well as preaching. Annie Merle assisted with his duties and sang in the Special Tabernacle Choir.

While in Indiana, World War II started and the young minister bundled up his wife and daughter and headed south—back home.

Annie Merle had been closed in by snow and ice with a young daughter, but never once complained. However, the light of heaven shined on her face when Forrest announced that they were returning to Texas!

The youth of the church gave them a farewell party and instead of gifts to pack and ship, gave them a love-offering. . .just the money they needed—their fare home.

Forrest went back to work for the South Central Council and they purchased a small three-room house. Annie Merle worked hard at making it a home, fashioning it into a dollhouse on the inside while Forrest manicured the lawn outside. God was good!

On the way to work one morning, the Lord spoke to the heart of the young minister. He was walking along, thinking that the Lord was soon to come and that he really needed to get out into the harvest field and win souls. He did not have the money to travel, so what could he do? Then the voice spoke, "Can't you have faith?" He looked around to see who spoke to him, but there was no one in sight. It was God dealing with him.

"Today I will resign and go," he said, and with tears streaming down his face, he related the story to Pastor Ford. Pastor Ford understood, saying, "I knew that it was about time for you to go, so I'll do everything I can to help you. Remember, you will have to have a home base, so

always feel free to come home. This church loves you!" Such good news!

When duty called, the little house was traded for a 1935 black Plymouth sedan, their very first car! They thought it rode like a dream.

The first venture now was to attend the District Conference in Conroe and let all pastors know that Forrest was again on the evangelistic field. The very last day of conference came, however, and not one minister had booked him for a revival.

"What are we going to do?" asked his wife.

"Go back to Kilgore," he replied. It seemed that their trip to conference was in vain. He thought perhaps he had missed the will of the Lord.

Then at dismissal, Pastor G. D. Harvey asked him to preach for him just as soon as he had an opening. Not wanting to act over-elated, Forrest told him that he had an opening at present if he wanted a revival that soon.

So from conference, they left for Nederland, Texas. He rode in one car and his wife and baby in another. They were to stay with some friends named Adams until Sunday so that they could begin the revival that night in Nederland. Here, though, their life took another turn!

A youth rally was scheduled in Beaumont at the Northend Pentecostal Church that afternoon, so they decided to attend. The evangelist was seated on the platform along with some other young ministers when some of the youth from Port Arthur entered. As Titus McDonald passed by, he spoke to Evangelist Ford. "Good afternoon, Pastor."

Astonished, Forrest looked at him and asked, "What on earth are you talking about?" Then added, "I'm not a pastor!"

"You are now," answered Titus. "As of this morning." Then grinning, he said, "Brother Dillon resigned and recommended that the church call you for their pastor. When the vote was taken, you were put in one hundred percent."

Forrest learned that they wanted him to come and be installed that night. Arrangements had to be made with Pastor Harvey to engage another evangelist.

The First Pentecostal Church of Port Arthur was a large church with a beautiful modern parsonage. It proved to be one of Forrest's most successful pastorates.

A great event took place here. Their second child, a boy, was born. Roy David is now married and the father of five lovely children: Anaka, Carmen, Jennifer, Farah, and Jason. His wife, Glenda, is a beautiful Christian woman, loved dearly by the entire family. Roy David and his family attend his father's church. Roy David is a public school music and choir teacher, and works with the music in the church.

Pastor Ford had nine young people from his church in Port Arthur to attend the Bible college in Milford, Texas. It was to this college that he and Annie Merle drove and returned with two of its graduates, J. T. and Bessie Pugh, to help them in the work at Port Arthur. A few years later, this couple returned to become pastor of the church, and they remain the best of friends.

Some of the very best years of the Fords' lives were spent in Conroe. Fond memories linger here. One winter, heavy snow covered the ground. Some of the young couples came by the parsonage with a boat tied to a car, using it for a sleigh. The Fords climbed aboard. They dragged the bottom completely out of the boat having such a great time! When Forrest and Annie Merle think of this today, they smile and say, "Those were the good old days."

They weathered many storms, trials, and afflictions while in Conroe, but one of the very hardest was that Roy David, at age seven, contacted bulbar polio and was in an iron lung. The doctors said that even if he lived, he could be a vegetable because his respiratory system was completely paralyzed. The Lord performed a miracle and he lived, blessed with perfectly normal health. The doctors called him the "wonder boy."

Prayer was their source of help. This was noised abroad as the radio station called Pastor Ford three times a day to get a report to announce on their news. Churches of other faiths joined with them in prayer. What a glorious day it was when the news went out over the air, "Roy David Ford has been pulled out of the lung for awhile and is steadily improving!" This certainly drew his father and mother closer and gave them an understanding to bear with others in their trials.

True love survives. . .it arises *"out of the depths."* Love for God, for others, and for one another. . .here was proof that their marriage was made in heaven.

After twelve years in Conroe, Forrest and Annie Merle moved to Houston to accept the church that Pastor Elmer Stanley and his wife, Myrtle, had begun. This church grew out of its facilities. It was eventually moved to Humble. Twenty-eight years have passed, and the Fords are still laboring for the Lord at Faith Tabernacle.

Courting along the banks of the Arkansas River September, 1937, Tulsa, Oklahoma.

Just before the wedding, April 3, 1938 at Annie Merle's Home.

Newlyweds in flower bed after wedding, 1938 Gilmer, Texas.

Behind Kilgore Church, after wedding, April 3, 1938.

Happiness·is. . .

. . .finding a blue-eyed Bug

By Nona Freeman

Depression throes still gripped the Southland in 1937. My dad deserted his family in late 1936, leaving me stranded at Arkansas A. & M. College at Monticello.

The ultimatum came after a lonely Christmas spent with two other destitute friends at the dormitory: "Leave the school premises before January 30th."

Where could I go?

My mother and five little brothers stayed with reluctant relatives who said plainly, "There isn't room for you here."

How could I get to—wherever?

145

I had not one cent. But my godly mother, Carrie Eastridge, spent hours on her knees while others slept in the home where she cooked and cleaned house for her board.

My roommate's cousin, Leigh Freeman, came to see her and found me sitting on the floor crying over my desperate situation, when I thought everyone had left. The sad story came out with her sympathy.

"Come to West Monroe and stay with me," she invited. "You can look for a job."

The "How" solution came a few days later with a belated Christmas card containing a five dollar bill. I rode the bus to Louisiana on a harrowing trip with a lecherous driver.

The next day, January 25, while I bent over a small trunk sorting my few possessions, I heard Leigh say, "If you'll get your head out of that trunk, I'd like you to meet Bug, my husband's brother. Bug, this is Nona. She's not an ostrich even though her head is out of sight!"

I straightened up to look into blue, blue eyes. Time slipped away. Something unfathomable and precious touched me. Griefs of recent traumas began to melt.

I thought, *I've waited all of my life for those blue eyes under that thatch of blond wavy hair.*

The moment stretched on and on—both of us wordless. Not so much an electrical charge held us as a bonding of mutual knowledge, "You are the *one*."

Leigh, always adept at aimless chatter, became more and more uncomfortable. "Well, for goodness' sake," she muttered and decided matters must be restored to normal. "If you two will come back to earth. . ." she grabbed Bug's arm and shook it, ending the enchanting moment.

Not really, for it became the beginning of enchantment, with continual schemes for time to be together. We married seven months later.

I believe in love. As partners working for Jesus, the God-ordained love born in our hearts that day has glowed for almost half a century—through storm and sunshine, rough or smooth ways, even through a few murky valleys.

Thank God for love.

Editor's Note: *"Bug and Nona" were married on August 26, 1937. Their ministry began in Portales, New Mexico, in 1939, leading them to the Rio Grande Valley, and then to Rosepine, Louisiana, in 1941. From there, they left to go to Africa in 1948. They were missionaries in South Africa for twenty-six years. Brother Freeman became Regional Supervisor for the Continent of Africa in 1972—a position he still holds that requires a continuous schedule of traveling for both of them.*

*The Freemans have five children, sixteen grandchildren, and at the time of this printing, they are anticipating their first great-grandchild. "God's way of leading and directing our footsteps are so **delicious!**" Sister Freeman wrote in the note accompanying her story. Read the rest of her story in her books **Bug and Me** and **Bug and Nona on the Go** published by Word Aflame Press.*

The Freeman Family.

Happiness is. . .

. . .living under His wings

By Ernest Holley and
Verba Joy Holley

When did "our" life as "one" begin? As far as Ernest and I are concerned, it began thirty-seven years ago. But as I look back now, I realize that the One who knows the end from the beginning was at the helm of our individual lives. He brought us together! Praise the Lord! He does all things well!

It seems like such a short time ago—like yesterday—that it all began. I suppose I was a typical young lady. I dreamed of marrying the perfect man. I didn't know a thing about "positive thinking" or "imaging." I wasn't even acquainted with the verse of Scripture: "All things are possible to him that believeth." But I knew what kind of person I wanted to marry.

As I look back now, I realize that I was rather naive. I mean, how in the world could a country girl like me captivate the "ideal" man I envisioned?

My ideal would be an extrovert—outgoing, friendly, jovial, and yes, even stockily built. He would also be a neat, well-groomed, kind gentleman.

"Now, really, Verba Joy, do you think you can find a guy with all those characteristics? Maybe, one or two of them—but *all* of them? Nobody's perfect, you know."

"Yes, I believe there is such a guy, somewhere. I don't know who he is and I don't know where he is. But I intend to find him."

"Well, even if you could find such a guy, do you think he would even look at you?"

From time to time these thoughts went through my mind. But since I was only seventeen years old, I figured I had plenty of time. I would just keep my eyes and ears open. And when such a fellow came into my life, I knew I would know it!

I graduated from Frankston High School in May, 1948. Frankston, Texas, was a very small town and there were few job opportunities. I persuaded my parents to permit me to move to Fort Worth, Texas, to look for a job. I lived with my older sister and her husband until I found a secretarial job. Shortly afterward, I rented a small apartment near my sister's home.

One evening in late summer of that same year, my sister called and invited me to her home. Her husband's first cousin, Ernest Holley, was visiting them. She wanted me to meet him. Since I didn't have any other plans, I went over.

After introductions, the four of us spent the evening playing cards. (Although Ernest's father was a Pentecostal pastor, neither he nor I were in the Pentecostal church.) As we laughed and talked, it dawned on me: "Hey, this is the one!"

This fellow seemed to have all the characteristics I had looked for in a man! He was a neat, well-groomed, kind, gentleman. He was outgoing, friendly, jovial and stockily built.

He had recently been discharged from the United States Navy. He was a good conversationalist—he could talk on *any* subject. I thought he was the most intelligent person in the whole world. (After thirty-seven years, I still think so!)

It was love at first sight for me! I was more than a little elated when he asked for my address at the end of the evening.

Letters began to arrive from different towns in West Texas. (His home was in Wichita Falls, but his job involved quite a bit of traveling.) Oh, how I enjoyed those letters— beautiful handwriting, beautiful phraseology, poetry! He could write as well as he could talk!

He rarely had visited his cousin before. But now, his visits became more and more frequent. In fact, it soon became a weekly occurrence, and each visit with his cousin included a date with me.

Our dates were usually with my sister and her husband—a foursome. Picnics, miniature golf, and evenings spent in my sister's home were typical dates. No chef could compare with her in preparing meals. Those were delightful times!

As the weeks went by, I became aware of a flaw in my ideal man. I never mentioned it to anyone. But he drank—especially when he was with my brother-in-law. To me, this was not altogether unacceptable. Yet I didn't approve. It was a flaw—that's all—a flaw! Otherwise, he was my ideal.

We had been dating only a short time when I learned that this jovial guy also had a very serious side. He had decided he wanted to marry me! I was thrilled! I wanted to marry him, too. But not right now. I was only seventeen. Earlier in my life I had made a commitment—to myself—that I would not marry until I was eighteen years old.

I knew he was the type of man I wanted to marry. I knew that I loved him. But I did not want to get married until after April 27, 1949, when I would be eighteen.

"And," I reasoned, "it's only five months away."

But he seemed to have his mind made up. He wanted to get married, now!

(He wasn't a religious man at the time. But the way he acted, he must have believed at least one verse of Scripture: "What thou doest, do quickly. . . ." He wanted to get married quickly!)

We didn't have a big "falling-out." There had been no cross words. There had been no big argument.

But his visits and letters began to get farther and farther apart. Finally, they ceased altogether. I was totally devastated! Did I make a big mistake? Should I have been so determined to have my own way, and keep a silly commitment I had made to myself?

I was tempted to contact him—write or call. But thirty-seven years ago, young ladies were taught that the man was to be the aggressive one. So I waited.

Months passed. Anger, pouting, crying, feelings of self-pity, poor self-image—all of the emotions such a situation can produce came into my being.

A cold, dismal winter passed.

Spring ushered in the long summer days.

I dated other fellows. But my mind was still on my "ideal." And I was certain there was only one ideal man for me, and that was Ernest Holley!

I checked the mailbox, expectantly. I listened for the telephone to ring. I kept expecting him to come to visit his cousin. But there were no letters, no phone calls, no visits—not a word!

Finally, on a cool, fall evening in 1949—what seemed like such a long time had only been a few months—there was a knock at my apartment door.

There he stood, on the porch!

My heart skipped. His first words were: "Will you marry me, and live under my wings so happily?"

This time I was more than ready to answer with a big resounding "YES!"

The next few days I was deliriously happy; I seemed to be floating in the clouds! The people with whom I worked didn't have to see the engagement ring on my finger; they knew by the way I looked that something had happened. It almost seemed like a dream; it was too good to be true. It was hard to believe that I—a country girl from Frankston—was engaged to the most intelligent, most wonderful man in the whole world!

The next few weeks were busy ones. I wanted Ernest to meet my family, and he wanted me to meet his. So the first available weekend my sister, her husband, Ernest and

I made a trip to Frankston. That was the first time I had seen Ernest nervous. He was more than a little reluctant to talk with my dad and ask for his approval of our marriage. But he had no need to worry—it was very obvious that Daddy liked him and approved. In fact, Daddy immediately began to treat him as "one of the boys."

The next weekend, Ernest took me to Wichita Falls to meet his family. Now it was my turn to be nervous. But they quickly made me comfortable, and welcomed me with open arms. I had never been around Pentecostal people before, and they made a profound impression on me. I was excited about becoming a part of this wonderful family.

Finally, with all the formalities out of the way, we were married on October 15, 1949. That has been over thirty-five years ago, and I have never doubted that Ernest Lee Holley was the "ideal" man for me. "God hath joined. . ." us together!

My Husband's Addendum

Memories, warm and beautiful, wafted through my mind as I read my wife's account of our courtship and marriage. I can remember a thousand details which are not easily verbalized. How could I express the emotions of my first glimpse of the loveliest young lady I had ever seen? Or, for that matter, how can I explain how she has grown lovelier with each passing day?

Anyway, I wanted to write an addendum. I want to try as best I can to convey another perspective to the union that is ours. You see, our marriage was, in fact, ordained of God. He had us in His plan, and it pleased Him to join us together even before we knew Him!

My cousin had told me she was pretty and had a great personality. After our first evening together, I found myself saying over and over, "The half was not told me!" Now, almost forty years later, I still maintain that to be true. The genuine laughter, the quick smile, the charming manner —all accentuated her loveliness. Amazingly enough, each beautiful attribute has become more and more pronounced!

Three years after our marriage, we moved to Wichita Falls, Texas, where we began to attend the church my father pastored. We were converted in the early part of 1953. Our lives took on new meaning. In the latter part of 1953, I was called to preach. We were active in every phase of the church.

In March, 1955, my wife and I entered a delapidated little building in Electra, Texas, to begin my first pastorate. With a prim little hat and gloved hands, she carried our seven-month-old son and led our three-year-old daughter through the side door, around a wood stove, and into a dismal sanctuary with plank pews. We had our first service. The old building had been unused for years and was in sad disrepair. (Three weeks later, we razed the building and poured a foundation for a new one.)

There, I began to see new dimensions of character, integrity, compassion, concern and devotion to God. Nine years later, I accepted another pastorate. In the meantime, we had adopted four children. When we arrived in LaMarque, Texas (all eight of us!), we had to enlarge the parsonage. Each time I'd watch her comb four heads of hair, prepare meals, play the organ in service, and apply band-aids to two rough-and-tumble boys, I'd stand in awe and admiration afresh! Not to mention teaching a Sunday school class and conducting the Ladies' Bible Study weekly—I still can't fathom the scope of her abilities.

Space won't permit me to relate how she adapted to Bible college administration. Along the way, she had earned several college credits and her knowledge of accounting was invaluable. Through two periods of Bible college administration, she counseled, taught, and developed a transcript system which secular colleges adopted for their use. No, space won't permit!

Now after eight years as the wife of a district superintendent, I can see how God has uniquely equipped this wonderful wife of mine. Insight and understanding are hers. She has experienced all the difficulties and perplexities of a minister's wife, yet her optimistic attitude has never dampened. An unswerving confidence in God emboldens and enriches my life. My love for her has been and yet is far, far more expansive than I ever thought it could be!

Her grace and poise still turn my head.

Her understanding during times of stress and perplexity is a heaven-sent balm.

Her glance across a crowded room can be reassuring.

Her hand on mine can make both long hours and long miles seem shorter.

Her attitude toward God and others overwhelms me.

Her industry amazes me, and her aptitude in the things of God inspire me.

God gave her to me! From the vantage view of the present, I not only recognize His hand in our lives in the past, I also look eagerly to the future. Together, under God, we can continue to grow in hope, faith and love!

Happiness is. . .

. . .a surprise first kiss

By Judy Hudson

Boys! How could anyone ever consider falling in love with such creatures? They had absolutely no manners, were always dirty and smelly and loved frogs, snails, worms, and tarantulas. I *knew;* I had two brothers. They were experts at forgetting their manners, forgetting to wash their hands, and they never threw away their chewing gum because they used it to bait their strings to catch another furry tarantula.

Boys. . .they gave me creeps! Who needed boyfriends anyway?

But my best friend Rachel had discovered boys, and

since she did not have any little brothers, she thought they were God's special gift to girls. It was very disgusting. She had no earthly idea what horrid creatures they were, and she was determined that it was time that the boys knew we existed. We were fourteen, and the most important subject discussed in our circles was "the boys," so I pretended to like them also.

What a relief when Daddy caught us flirting! "I will not allow you to date until you are sixteen," he informed me. So we were wasting our efforts.

Sweet sixteen came quite soon and by then all my friends were in love. They made their boyfriends sound like such dreamboats and wonderboys that I decided it was time I found out about this special breed of boys. The day I became sixteen, my father and I were in Albuquerque, New Mexico, where my father, Reverend C. L. Abbott, was speaking at a series of special services. We were staying at the pastor's home. They had two handsome sons, and one had just become sixteen.

Since it was my birthday and we were excited about being sixteen, we decided to celebrate. I informed my father that I was going across town to a youth gathering and the pastor's son informed his parents of the same. Neither of us bothered to tell our parents that we were going *together.* We were sixteen and if our parents had declared that we could not date until we were sixteen, we felt it stood to reason that that meant we *could* date when we *were* sixteen.

The young man and I had a great time and joined other teens for a coke after the service. We were both shocked when we arrived back at his home and our parents were waiting up for us, unhappy with the way we had started our plunge into the wonderful world of dating! But I was the envy of all my friends for awhile.

That summer I decided that Rachel was right—boys could be fairly nice creatures. We liked them all and tried to please them all. Some of them were so skinny that if they turned sideways they disappeared and others were so short that they had to walk on tiptoes and crane their necks as far up as possible to try to reach our heights, while we went about with slumped shoulders to hide our enormous heights of five feet, five inches!

The next year, Susan, my cousin, decided that Rachel and I needed some special instructions. We just were not sophisticated enough in our tactics and choices. "You're wasting precious time on boys," she informed us, "when you should be looking for *men*."

"You were born preacher's daughters, and that qualifies you to be preacher's wives!" she said. "But if you keep dating these inexperienced boys, you are never going places in life!"

"I'm going to marry a 'flaming evangelist,' " she concluded, "with his ministry established and his pocketbook well lined!"

Now that we had decided to be "sophisticated," we had to put our hair on top of our heads and dress like "older" women. We dug out our mothers' hats and the highest heeled shoes we could find. Our shoulders became perfectly straight and our noses a little higher on our faces. Overnight we became twenty-one and ready for "the best"!

About a month later, we went to the camp meeting in Amarillo, Texas. It is difficult to imagine our embarrassment when our fathers checked into a cheap motel near the campgrounds! We were humiliated! We just knew they had ruined all our carefully made plans, so we got our heads together and came up with some new strategies. We decided that after our dates, when our young men took us back to the motel, we would have them let us off at the nice, fancy motel down the street. Then after the "goodbyes" had been said and they had left, we would walk down to the "ratty" motel that our folks had chosen. We did just that!

Our "flaming evangelists" came in from Oklahoma, Texas, Louisiana, and Colorado, but for some reason they still treated us like little sisters. We finally gave up and started dating boys our own age again. Anyway, Daddy found out about our tricks and said, "Judy, all you girls are doing with your fancy clothes and hats is scaring the boys off!" He said we'd have more fun being sixteen and letting our hair down. So much for "flaming evangelists." Daddy turned our dreams to ashes! He was not going to let me date "older men" anyway, so I had an excuse to turn down all those dates that I was going to get—and be my age again.

Daddy really was a lot of fun. I had discovered that he was probably the best friend I ever had, so I confided everything in him. He always had the best advice, and I found out just how clever he really was when I tried some of his advice and it worked. He taught me what boys were looking for in a girl. When I came from my room "dressed to the teeth," he would say, "Go tone it down, Judy. You've got to be more subtle. You don't want to make the guy afraid to take you to a hamburger joint if that's all he can afford."

He advised me never to date a guy seriously that I would not consider marrying. "You marry one of the boys you date," he said.

"Watch the way a boy treats his mother," he told me, "because men treat their wives like they treat their mother." So if I saw a boy mistreat his mother, or be disrespectful, it was "So long, nice knowing you" because I wanted to be cherished.

I let Daddy read all my love letters and then he helped me answer them correctly. He advised me, "Never answer a 'mushy' letter with mush. Letters are incriminating evidence and can prove very embarrassing when faced later." When I obeyed that advice, I proved him right; when I didn't, things got rather disgusting.

At the grand old age of nineteen, I had decided that I was destined to be an "Old Maid." I had dated my share of preachers' sons and saints' sons and the lovebug had just not bitten. I spent two years in Bible college and developed a lot of close friendships with young men and had many big brothers—but still love had not come my way. I finally decided that this "love" business was just for the birds, and I was going to have to choose a mate like one chooses a show quality horse, by his attributes and breeding and learn to love him later. So I began to look at the lists.

Graduation night at college came. I had turned down invitations to date afterwards because I was waiting for Mr. Special to ask me, and he didn't. I was heart-broken, so I went to the phone and called Daddy.

Daddy listened as I cried and told him that the only boy that I really cared for had let me down. Then he quietly said, "Judy, you have not yet met the man God intends for your life."

"But, Daddy, you just don't understand," I cried.

"Yes," he said, "I understand. There are certain stages that you go through in life to prepare you for real love and proper choices. Without these you would not recognize true qualities and characteristics in another person. These lessons are good for you."

This was one time that I felt that my Dad had stayed out in the sun too long! But Daddy was the authority, so I listened to him. He decided that I should leave the next day and he arranged for me to spend the summer with his father, Reverend Mack Abbott. I was so excited that I soon forgot to mope!

Granddad always had good-looking young men in his church. There was an Air Force base nearby, and between Granddad's preaching and Grandma's good cooking, they didn't stand a chance. They learned to serve God along with their country! Granddad already had five beautiful granddaughters in his church to lure them in, but look out—another was on her way!

Saturday morning bright and early, I headed for Roswell, New Mexico, to spend the summer with my grandparents and my five beautiful cousins. I planned to give them plenty of competition with the boys. To say the least, I was excited!

Daddy made me promise to date any Christian boy that asked me out, and Granddad promised that my heart would mend in no time! On the way, I checked it out. It was surprising what a little bit of distance and a few days could do for your heart. When I walked into Granddad's house late Sunday night, it was full of young people. One young man with black curly hair decided immediately that it was his responsibility to see that I had a nice summer. I had a terrific summer and decided that I wasn't cut out to be an "old maid" after all!

Granddad took us cousins all with him to sing and help in a special revival he held in South Texas. We had the time of our lives! Then we went to the camp meeting. One night a "flaming evangelist" asked me out, but he was more than I bargained for. So the next evening when he asked me out, Susan (who liked "flaming evangelists") offered to take him off my hands. When we went out to the car to go for a drive, I got in the car with her date and she got in with mine. They both were a little startled that we had conveniently forgotten which one had asked who, but neither of them had the nerve to straighten us out, so we got away with it. We thought it was great fun until my father, who had come for the camp meeting, took a liking to the young man that I had done the "great switch" with! I knew by the way he was talking that he was ready to arrange my marriage, and that the Lord and I were going to have to work fast to get me out of this one.

Sure enough, I was in hot water! Daddy began asking very leading questions. Like, "What do you feel about this young man? Don't you think he has great qualities?"

"Certainly, Daddy, but give me a chance," I answered. "I've never let a man kiss me, but at least with some, I've felt certain emotions from a special look, or sensations when he held my hand. But this guy wasn't even my date. He was Susan's! And he's so shy that he can hardly look me in the eye! He leaves me cold. I went with him because at least I didn't have to fight him off."

Poor Daddy! He was giving up on me. Every guy he liked was either too "fast" for me or too "slow." He then gave me a regular discourse on how love grows after marriage and said, "You need to pick a husband for his qualities!"

After camp, we went back to Granddad's. The young man that I had begun dating went to my father and asked for my hand. So Daddy asked me to stop dating him since he was serious and I was not. Daddy was concerned enough with me that he almost made me go home with him, but I begged to just stay the rest of the month before going back to Bible college. I was having so much fun that he could not resist me. Besides, the young man that *he* so much approved of was coming to see me in one week.

After Daddy left to go back to California that Saturday, I went over to Granddad's church to pray. "Lord, I sure need Your help. Surely there's someone special for me that wouldn't leave me cold," I told the Lord. I felt terrific when the Holy Ghost came; surely love in the natural was like the Holy Ghost. "Besides, God, if You don't, Daddy will—and his choice may preach like Paul and sing like an angel, but I feel like a Methodist when they are around!"

After talking with the Lord, I felt too heavenly-minded to go out with the other girls, so for the first Saturday that summer I stayed home with Granddad.

Granddad was very special and I loved visiting with him and Grandmother. Each night that summer when I would come in from a date, Granddad would be sitting up waiting on us girls. He didn't bother the other girls about their dates, but he had special instructions for me. He had to give an account to my father.

Each evening he would be sitting in his recliner reading when I came through the door. He would look over his spectacles and say, "Judy, did you let that boy kiss you tonight?"

And I would always grin and say, "Not tonight, Grandpa, maybe tomorrow night!" He loved it and I loved him. This Saturday night I told him I was going to stay home and kiss him.

Sweet twenty and never been kissed—and some of my cousins had never been missed! I truly hoped that there wasn't something drastically wrong with me! I decided to ask Granddad if there was something wrong with me. He looked over his "specs" and said, "You just haven't met a real man yet. He won't take 'No' for an answer!"

Sunday morning, August 5, 1964, I felt a little homesick. Dad and Mom had returned to California, I had broken my best boyfriend's heart because I wouldn't get serious with him, and I was tired of being single. That Sunday morning my hair would not do a thing. I was supposed to be early to do the secretary job for the youth class and I was already late. I was very tempted to crawl back in bed, but I had been taught better than that, so I pulled my hair back in a "granny-knot" and headed across the street to church.

The class was full of young people. I didn't look at anyone, but headed straight to the desk. I took out the record book and started taking roll. When I looked up, I noticed that three new servicemen from the Air Force Base were in attendance and one handsome critter was already snoozing (which was not at all flattering to our youth teacher). I must have giggled out loud because he opened his eyes and looked straight at me and began to grin. The impact I felt was unreal! It was as if everyone else in the room disappeared and we were alone. He would not look away and I felt spellbound and strangely uncomfortable, yet comfortable at the same time. I had never had anyone control my emotions like he seemed to be doing with a look!

Finally, I realized that we were staring and the room was full of people who were now watching us. So I took my record book and left the class. Later, I went to the auditorium to play the piano for Granddad's adult class, and shortly the youth class joined us for worship service. When I looked out into the audience, that handsome creature was staring at me again with that look in his eyes, right in church! I looked away because my heart was in my throat again. I was missing notes on the piano and Granddad was wondering where my mind was! He didn't know that one of the world's most sought-after bachelors had just decided to change his way of life. . .and that one of his granddaughters had decided to help him.

Immediately after the service, my favorite cousin and best friend came directly to the piano. "Judy," she said, "did you see the new servicemen that came in this morning?"

"Of course," I responded.

"Well," she said, "The tall, good-looking one is Tommy Hudson from Oklahoma City. He's been stationed in Alaska for over a year, and recently sent here to finish his last two years of duty with the Air Force. A friend from Oklahoma wrote me and told me that he was due here, and, furthermore, young lady, this guy is mine! You keep away from him!"

I just smiled and said to myself, "Sorry, little lady, you're too late. He's already staked his claim."

My cousins invited all the young men to join us for dinner and sample Grandmother's good cooking. Tommy followed me with his beautiful blue eyes, and although we did not even speak when introduced, we both knew our time had come. All through dinner, he chatted with his friends and with my cousins, but when he looked at me, he spoke volumes without saying a word.

Granddad always went downtown for a jail service after dinner on Sundays. He invited Tommy, Ronnie, and Glen to go with us that day. We took our accordions, guitars, and songbooks and four of us girls rode in the back of the boys' car to show them the way. When the others started into the city building and were out of hearing, Tommy called me by name and asked me to wait on him. That was the first time he had spoken to me. Then he said, "If I come back to church tonight, will you take me out afterwards and buy me a coke?"

I laughed at him and said, "You come back and we'll see!"

That night we had a marvelous service, but playing the piano until the last one leaves the altar has its disadvantages. In the back of the church, dates were being set. Tommy and his friends were surrounded by my five beautiful cousins (and all the other pretty girls in the church). Finally, I walked back to the back of the church to join the crowd. Mr. Blue-eyes did not disappoint me. He stepped through the middle of all the beautiful young ladies and came to meet me, taking my arm. None questioned his right to do so, although a few mouths dropped open in surprise.

Well, I had met my match and he left me tongue-tied, which was unnatural for me. I had always prided myself in being able to handle the situation and be left in control, but I was definitely out of control.

There didn't seem to be much need for words that night. I felt heavenly just sitting beside him! Everyone else seemed out of focus and far away. I had heard of dizzy blonds; I was dizzy and I wasn't a blond! We communicated very well that night. Tommy talked and I agreed.

When we started home, we rode in the back seat of his friend's car. Tommy said something to me and I was so content just to sit next to him that I didn't answer. So he reached over and ran his finger down my nose. When, as a natural reaction, I raised my face to look at him, he kissed me very gently. My lands! I felt tingly all the way to my toes! Besides, I didn't kiss boys, much less on the first date! But believe it or not, I had just been soundly kissed and there was nothing cold about it. I was afraid I had just met that man that my grandfather had told me about!

I didn't know it, but Tommy had called home and talked to his mother that day and told her that he had at last met the girl he intended to marry. She could not believe her ears; neither could his dad. Their bachelor son had bit the dust! His dad was so thrilled at the prospect of seeing his son settle down that he drove five hundred miles from Oklahoma City to Roswell the next day to bring Tommy a car and meet this magic girl.

When I started across the street on Tuesday evening for service, I noticed a strange car from Oklahoma. And stranger yet, when I entered the sanctuary, I was met by Tommy and immediately introduced and hugged by an older gentleman that I learned was Tommy's father. These Hudson men mean business and they don't waste time once they make up their minds! Tommy and I took his father to the bus depot after church so that he could go back to Oklahoma to go to work the next day, leaving Tommy his car so that he could finalize his decision.

My grandmother was a little upset because things were moving so fast. She talked to me, worrying about what my father would think and do when he heard the news. Grandfather just grinned and looked over his specs, asking no questions. That's how I knew that he was on my side.

Tommy soon won Grandmother over. He bragged on her cooking and showed up each night at suppertime from Wednesday on just to prove his sincerity. She could not resist that beautiful smile. By silent consent we decided to put Daddy on ice for a few more days.

Thursday evening, Tommy and I left Granddad's house and went for a walk. We strolled down the hill, then down Thirteenth Avenue across a creek that ran through a lovely natural park, full of gorgeous trees and greenery. Flowers grew everywhere; the air was fresh and clean. In fact, the whole world had taken on a heavenly atmosphere.

Tommy began to ask some very leading questions. "Do you have any other boyfriends?"

"Of course," I answered.

He then proceeded to ask me about each one and it was as if he was discounting each one like so much excess baggage as we went along.

"I have a date Saturday with a young preacher that's driving from Albuquerque to see me," I then told him.

He said quietly, as he put his arm around me, "You might as well tell him goodbye when he comes, because he won't feel too comfortable with me along—and I will be there, because you are going to marry me. You won't have time for anyone else."

I felt a little indignant, wondering how I was going to handle this situation. We had known each other for five whole days and already the guy was telling me what to do with my dates. He hadn't asked me to marry him, he had simply informed me that it was going to occur! But when I looked up to defy him and saw those beautiful blue eyes, I melted. Why fight it? I was too weak and this feeling was too good. I had met the man my grandfather had warned me about—and it looked as if I might as well start enjoying being told what to do.

By the end of the second week, my grandmother had learned that Tommy and I were serious enough that we were making plans for marriage. She decided that my father must be told. To say the least, we all dreaded the prospect of informing him that the little daughter he had left to finish out the month peacefully with her grandparents had stepped into a new world with a new man and it was someone he did not know.

Daddy was stunned! Then he hit the ceiling and ordered me to come home immediately. I was terribly upset. I tried to explain my feelings to him, but how do you explain love? Finally, after talking to him and crying my heart out, I was about to give up. Then I said, "Daddy, I can't explain this sudden thing, but you must understand I love him more than I do you."

There was dead silence on the other end. Then I heard Granddad on the other phone say, "Son, you are going to have to listen to her. This is all in the will and plan of God."

Daddy said, "How can you say that, Dad? Only two weeks ago I left her there and she wasn't serious about anyone and now you expect me to accept a total stranger with my daughter!"

"Come meet him for yourself before you make any

more threats, then we'll decide what to do," Granddad answered. Dad agreed.

Then Tommy tried to talk to him. He asked Daddy for permission to marry me and Daddy said, "Don't ask my permission; I don't have a chance. My daughter just told me that she loves you more than she loves me and my father gave me orders to drive all the way to New Mexico to shake your hand in congratulations!"

During the next few days, Tommy and I learned to pray together. We felt we were facing the lion's den. Daddy had promised to show up anytime. Only a girl that is very close to her father would understand how it feels to be breaking ties with her father for the man she loves. I knew that God could help Daddy to love Tommy. He had started this work in my life at my request and I knew it was His Will for a father to approve his daughter's marriage, so I asked Him to finish the work.

I woke up a few days later to find my precious father was there. He was still very distant and angry with me. The closer it got to the time for Tommy to come, the more uptight Daddy became. He finally had me in tears. My face was swollen and my hair was in big pink rollers. Daddy said, "Good! If he comes in and sees you crying and in rollers, he'll run the other way!"

At that moment, Tommy walked in the front door. He came straight over to me, put his arms around me, and kissed me—right in front of Daddy and said, "Sir, I think she's beautiful anyway, anytime. . .I love her."

Daddy was rather speechless for a moment, then he started grinning and shook hands with my beloved. From then on when he spoke to me about Tommy, it was, "What a lucky gal you are to find such a great guy!"

Tommy soon had Daddy deciding how soon it would be convenient for Daddy to get me to the altar and into Tommy's arms permanently. They became the best of friends and from then on, I had *two* men agreeing on how to run my life!

Our wedding date was set for November 24, 1964. We had known each other for little more than three months when I floated down the aisle on my father's arm to start my new life with Tommy. I felt that I had known him since birth. The brief courtship had been the happiest days of my life.

The wedding was beautiful. And as we knelt for Granddad's blessings, Tommy's new shoes said, "S O S" and "Please Help Me!" on the soles. Compliments of his friends. We didn't mind one bit that they had fun. The Limburger cheese and the potato in the exhaust pipe were a little too much, but we survived. When we got to our mountain resort room and opened our suitcases, all our things were sewed flat and piled with rice, but we didn't mind—we had each other. My beloved was mine and I was his and all we needed was a few verses from Solomon.

We felt that marriage was heaven on earth. For months our friends gave us up for a lost cause because we always had a way of disappearing so that we could be alone.

Tommy began to feel his call to the ministry during our second year of marriage. And I soon discovered that I had a "flaming evangelist"! He was my pride and joy. There was none in the world like him, nor would there ever be. God gave us a beautiful little son during our second year of marriage and we felt our joy was complete. Since then, we have had two beautiful little girls who give their daddy a run for his money.

Tommy and I just celebrated our twentieth anniversary. We still have so much fun together! In fact, we are still just like a couple of kids when we can go home, lock the doors, and close out the world.

We've faced our hard times and bad times, but the good times so outweigh the bad! Together we've faced the loss of a beautiful little baby boy, and we were able to see him in the arms of our Lord. God's comfort has always surrounded us. When we had our misunderstandings and thought our marriage might tumble down, we found our answer in each other's arms and in the arms of the Lord as we let the tears wash away the pain and sweep our souls clean.

Together with the Lord we have been able to raise up a marvelous revival church for His name sake. Tommy has served as District Youth President and is now serving as Arizona Home Missions Director and National Indian Coordinator.

God has blessed our lives with His fulness and given us much undeserved honor. Tommy is away from home often, and sometimes I yearn for the simple life that we had together when we were first married. But I know that I can't look back. Life is always forward. So we make the most of our time together.

Life is what a person makes it, and we don't ever intend for ours to get boring. I married the greatest man on the earth and I'll never let him forget it. I never get tired of being awakened in the morning and told that I am as beautiful as the day he married me. He may be blind, but please, don't ever awake my love. . .let him dream on.

Engagement picture, November, 1964.

The Hudsons' family.

Happiness is. . .

. . .five minutes on the front porch

By Imogene Kilgore

NOTICE:
Revival
Beginning July 4
Evangelist James Kilgore

The thoughts of my eighteen year old mind were on pursuing my immediate career. Being private secretary to a bank officer afforded certain esteem in my hometown of Sherman, Texas, more than thirty years ago. This professional pursuit was not purposefully planned, however. Only two weeks earlier, some friends and I were college bound. At the last moment, I had inexplicably decided not to go. So I had entered the business world.

High school days had been spent routinely—studying, dating, attending church. I loved God and had sought to find my place in His plan. I loved God's Word, and even though lacking musical talent, I wanted to serve Him. A spiritual maturing occurred during that senior year, although the implications were not yet revealed.

So there I was, pounding the typewriter. "When will God send His message concerning my future?" I subconsciously wondered.

Our pastor, Brother and Sister Lamb, having no children of their own, had sort of "adopted" me and I enjoyed spending time with them. When I gave them a studio picture, they promptly displayed it in their living room. They were my friends.

When it was announced that the young preacher was scheduled to begin a revival for our church that July 4th, I made no special "preparation" for the service that summer evening because I was unfamiliar with his name. After all, this was East Texas where his fame had not yet spread. (Later, I learned that he was with his parents when they conducted a great revival in our city. He was five years old and I was three months; apparently we had ignored each other completely!)

On the first night of the revival, my aunt and I went into the church and were seated. Just then, *he* walked in. Boom! I could hardly breathe. It was as if he were a long lost friend! I could not take my eyes off him, and he watched me, too. In my mind, throughout the service, I knew he was exactly who I wanted to marry! *Marry?* We had not yet met, much less dated. How could I so positively know I wanted to marry him? The world stood still.

After church, he glanced my direction. I hurried to the door and onto the parking lot. I wanted him to wonder who I was and where I was, so I sat in the car waiting for my aunt. I did not even meet him.

But upon arriving home, the excitement engulfed me. I immediately awakened my parents and announced to them: "I saw the boy tonight whom I am going to marry." They laughed. But I insisted, "You watch, that's him. I'm going to marry him."

After service the next night, I still had that excited feeling. I lingered a bit longer and he was waiting at the front door. We spoke and shook hands. I cannot describe the feeling that went between us. Neither of us could quit smiling.

Earlier this evangelist had inquired about my picture in the pastor's home. "Is that your married daughter?"

"No, she is not our daughter. She is a girl from our church," Brother Lamb replied.

"Is she married?"

"No."

He was impressed by the picture and being so conscientious, he called his girl friend, whom he had been dating regularly, to break off their relationship.

When he indicated that he did not date girls who were dating already, I assured him that I was definitely meeting that qualification.

"If you will not date until the end of the revival, I would like to date you."

The next day my good friend, with whom I had walked to school and ridden to work, came to take me to the bank.

"Woody," I said, "I can't ride with you."

"Why?"

"I must be very careful; there's this boy I'm interested in and he doesn't want me to be near anybody else."

Quite bewildered, Woody drove away and cast a disbelieving glance over his shoulder. So I rode the bus to work every day. Once a group of friends offered a ride. I declined with, "Thank you, but I have other plans. . . ." And, did I ever!

About ten days later, James asked the pastor for permission to speak to me for five minutes on the front porch of the parsonage. His first words were, "Will you marry me?" And my first words were, "Yes, I sure will." I must admit at that "romantic" moment I did expect some symbol of affection, but to my dismay we simply shook hands as he said, "Lord bless you."

With our future together thus committed, we returned to the sanctuary, waving all the while to church members as they left the parking lot.

On the last night of the revival, July 30, we went on our first date. It was so thrilling! This was the happiest moment of my life. When we returned home, I just knew that he was going to kiss me. After all, we had been engaged for nearly two weeks. I saw him coming, and knew it was going to be—but it happened so fast that I almost missed it.

We were happily engaged and it was a whole new life. When he asked my dad for permission to marry me, the reply was, "Son, you're a good boy. But you can't afford her." But he could.

Other people called to advise him negatively: "That girl was not reared in a preacher's home. She knows nothing of the ways of the ministry. She doesn't even play the accordion and sing. You could ruin your ministry by marrying her. . . ."

So I immediately bought an accordion, intending to master it within record time. But I did not learn and I still cannot play one.

"James," I said, "I don't blame them for thinking those things. But I promise that you won't be sorry for taking a chance on me. You can establish the rules for life and I'll live by them. Whatever you say is what I will do." And I meant it from my heart.

My promise was unnecessary, though, because he loved me so much that no one could sway his decision. It was settled.

Six weeks later we were married. We had planned a small wedding in my home because I was too timid to walk down the aisle of a church where people would turn and look at me. Little did I know how many such walks through the church I would be taking in the future! Our few close friends turned into a large assembly of people. They filled the yards and packed into the house. I could barely crowd through to the dining room for the ceremony.

With our $30, we newlyweds traveled to Dallas, sixty miles from my hometown. We managed to find a service to attend for each of the three evenings of our honeymoon.

Pastoring churches became our life. We spent almost eight years in Paris, Texas, and twenty-seven years in Houston, Texas.

From a breathtaking, story-book courtship until now, James did establish some rules which I have lived by. But they are no longer rules; they are in my heart. God was so good to give me the greatest man in the world. Happiness is. . .five minutes on the front porch. . .and a handshake!

Happiness is. . .

. . .being the President's wife

By Vera Kinzie

Romance is defined as a love affair. It can be a spontaneous and exciting relationship or a natural and growing appreciation of an individual. Life-long happiness and fulfillment can be the result of either.

I was born and reared on a farm in northern Indiana. When I was seven years old, the farm next to ours was sold to a Mr. Kinzie, a stock buyer, who owned a meat market in Bremen, Indiana. We were soon to discover that the Kinzies had a young girl and boy. Great! Now we'd have some new playmates—a stone's throw away! The girl, Lauretta, was ten months older than I and the boy,

Fred, was seven months older than my brother, Noble.

In those days we children were allowed to play together once or twice a week and then only for a specified time—such as from 1:30 p.m. to 4:00 p.m. We developed into close friends. Lauretta taught me to play paper dolls, cutting the pictures out of the Sears and Roebuck catalogue. The boys had their own games too! One thing I remember well—the boys were so aggravating that we had many a quarrel. They would go by and blow our paper dolls away. We despised them!

We all went to the same school and personally I paid little attention to Fred. He was just my brother's playmate! This was status quo with me until I was a freshman in high school. One day a group of us girls were looking out the second floor windows of our school, watching the boys play basketball on the school's outdoor court. I noticed that the "neighbor boy" had grown tall and slim and was very nice looking and was also a good basketball player. That started the romance!

It had its "ups and downs"! When I was a senior I went to the senior banquet with Ralph, our class president; when Fred was a senior he went to his banquet with Helen, a very pretty girl. Our romance was at times tempestuous and also amusing!

Brother Kinzie likes to tell of the time we were in a Sunday school class. Of course, we were sitting side by side. We were about fifteen or sixteen at the time. The teacher asked Fred, "What are you planning to do in your life?"

Straightening up in his seat and with a twinkle in his eye, he replied, "Be the president of the United States of America."

I remember our teacher vividly as she had black curly hair and a cute "side-ways smile"—and with that "smile" she turned to me and asked, "And Vera, what plans do you have for your life?"

"I want to be the president's wife!" I remarked mischievously.

She broke into a laugh! She lived to see us married and expressed her approval.

I always thought a person shouldn't marry the first fellow she dated, so on several occasions we stopped dating—and dated others. But it wouldn't be long until we would be back together again, seeing qualities in each other that we admired above others. Really, our relationship developed over several years. We noted that we had the same ideas about the movie stars we liked, we attended the same church, we enjoyed sports, we liked Zane Grey's novels, and our families were very much alike. One day my father said, "You'd better look twice at that young man; he's all right!"

During our courting days the Pentecostal experience was introduced into our family. Sister Bertha Mangun, a neighbor, had received the gift of the Holy Ghost and convinced my aunt Effie, another neighbor, of its truth.

My mother was furious! She declared it was a disgrace to the family! This went on until midsummer when I developed a felon on a finger and my mother, realizing that the infection was dangerous, said, "Well, go over to your aunt and have her pray for you, if that religion is so wonderful!" Fred knew of the infection too, so I went and my aunt shouted as she prayed for me, thankful that we were "breaking down" our prejudices. I was healed and Fred and I realized God had performed a miracle. We began discussing this "new religion" but at the time did nothing about it. We were agreed even in religion, what more could one ask?

We were married several years following this experience, and we were both convinced that Acts 2:38 was the truth! After being married one and one-half years, we gave our hearts to God and somehow I knew that someday he would be a minister.

Our life together has been one of contentment and security. We have respected the qualities of character found in each other—and after fifty years of married life we are continually made aware of new attributes of disposition and personality in each other. He was my first and last date!

Happiness is. . .

. . .a laughing matter

By Leatrice Lamb

I had just turned away from the casket and started down the aisle when I saw him sitting in the back with his brother.

William saw me, too, and turning to his brother, said, "That girl is going to be my wife!" It was a case of mistaken identity. He thought I was from Sherman, Texas.

My pastor's mother-in-law had died and several people from our church were attending her funeral in Waco. William was my pastor's nephew.

"Did Leatrice come to the funeral?" William asked his uncle.

"There she is," Brother Lamb replied, pointing to

me—the very girl William had "chosen" to be his wife!

After the graveside service, we talked for awhile and he told me that he would be preaching a revival in Eastland, a short distance from my hometown of Ranger, during the summer and would see me then.

Since I had no car, a girlfriend offered me transportation, and we attended that revival regularly. After service each night, we would converse. And on one of these nights, he asked me to marry him. . . but when he asked me, he sort of *laughed. "What sort of proposal is this?"* I wondered, not sure how to take it.

Following the Eastland revival, my pastor asked his nephew to preach a revival in Ranger. William's brother, James, who played and sang, joined him.

"We'll be there Monday morning," they told their uncle.

However, they decided to go to his home after service Sunday night.

When they got to Ranger, they dismissed the one who had given them a ride with a generous thanks, and put their luggage on the porch of the darkened house.

They knocked and knocked and called and called, but no one responded. Finally, they decided to go to the window and knock on it to rouse their sleeping uncle.

Awakening from sleep, Brother and Sister Lamb heard the commotion by their bedroom window. Brother Lamb looked out the window and saw the two faces. There had been reports of burglars in the neighborhood; they decided someone was trying to break into their home.

"Get under the bed, wife, and I'll call the police!"

As Brother Lamb went to the telephone to call the police, Sister Lamb raised up to see if she could see anything.

"Wife, *get under the bed* before you get your dome knocked off!"

Sister Lamb had aluminum foil over the diamond-shaped pane in the front door. Her curiosity got the better of her and as she lifted the foil to peek, it slipped and fell, leaving her staring at two dark shapes. Startled, she hurriedly tried to replace the foil!

Sounds of sirens and squealing tires broke the night's silence. The policeman jumped from his car, starting toward the two bewildered young men with his club and his gun drawn.

"Uncle Esbee! Uncle Esbee! Let us in! It's William and James!"

The door swung open. "It's all right, Bill," Brother Lamb assured the policeman. "These are my nephews." Bill was a friend of Brother Lamb's, and they all had a good laugh over the "burglars."

On Monday morning, my pastor called William into his study. "William, I heard that you proposed to one of my girls while I was gone on vacation."

"Yes, sir."

"She said she didn't know if you were serious or not, because you *laughed* when you asked her."

(William laughed because he was bashful and didn't know what else to to.)

Then Brother Lamb said, "If you're serious, I'm all for it and will do anything I can to help you have a happy marriage, but if you're not, I'd rather cancel the revival and have you pack your bags and leave, because I don't want the girl hurt."

William decided it was time to become *really* serious.

During the revival, we talked and sometimes went out with the other young people, but we never had a date alone even though he was eighteen and I was nineteen and we were engaged.

William's next revival was in Kountze with Brother Speer. When Brother Speer realized that William was getting regular letters in feminine handwriting, he would go to the mailbox early and return to awaken William with, "I've got a sweet letter for you."

William returned to Ranger to work until we were married, rooming with his aunt and uncle. He would visit me as often as possible, but if he happened to stay later than eleven o'clock, there would be headlights in the driveway!

On September 28, 1963, we were married in Ranger, Texas, by our pastor, Brother J. E. Lamb. We had no car and no money to buy one, so Brother Lamb took the money William had paid him for room and board and bought us a green 1948 Chevrolet.

The young people of the church were laying plans to throw us in Lake Leon after the wedding. They had disengaged the distributor of our '48 Chevy. But it was "Uncle To The Rescue" when he happened to hear them planning the mischief. He slipped up behind William and me. "Jump in the back seat of my car when I start the engine!" he said.

He took off, leaving the youth scrambling to their cars in hot pursuit.

Brother Lamb took us to a restaurant in Eastland and, while we were eating, our pursuers came within one block of the restaurant before turning around and going back to Ranger.

Now, almost twenty-three years and three "little

Lambs" later, we're still living happily. . .*even* after.

Leatrice in Ranger before wedding William.

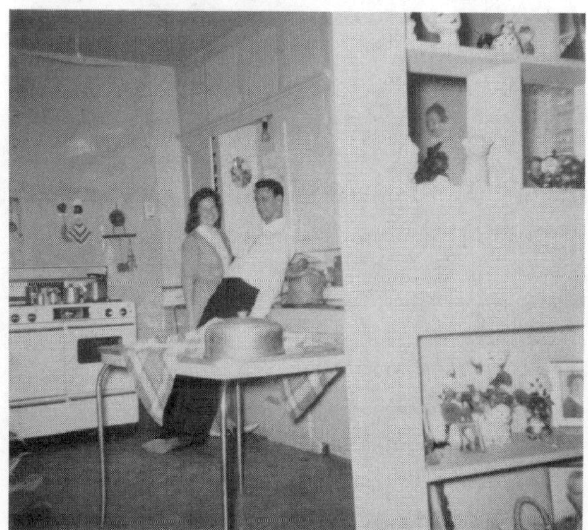

Dating scene. Doing dishes together at the home of Pastor Lamb.

Our first car 1948 Chevrolet.

William and Leatrice holding quilt presented to them as wedding gift by church ladies.

Happiness is. . .

. . .never "never"

By LaVerne Lindley

"**I** will remain a widow the rest of my life before I'll marry a preacher!" I told my pastor, Brother E. W. Caughron, when he teased me about an eligible minister.

"You'll wind up marrying one," he replied.

"Never."

I was widowed at the tender age of nineteen. My husband, J. B. "Tump" Bohannan, was killed in a well drilling accident after only one brief year of marriage.

I had *four* sisters married to preachers, plus a cousin (Arthur Clanton), a brother, and two nephews who were in the ministry—and two nieces who married preachers.

Who could blame me for saying "never"?

I spent several years after my husband's death in the gospel work, assisting in revivals and new works, helping with the music, singing, or whatever I could do to be a blessing in God's harvest field. After my mother passed away, I kept Dad's home going until 1963.

In 1955, one of my sisters, Louella, also lost her husband in a car accident, and I went to Houston to help her and her two-year-old baby through the tragedy and days of bitter loneliness that followed.

Several of my friends, sisters, and especially a niece, LaJoyce Martin, felt that I should remarry, and often found someone they thought "good husband material," only to be told, "No, thank you!"

In 1961, my brother-in-law assisted in the funeral of Reverend Perry Lindley's wife. Sometime later, my sister said to Louella and me, "I have Brother Lindley picked out for one of you."

I said, "Lou can have him."

Lou said, "LaVerne can have him."

And neither of us had even met him!

("They just tossed me back and forth like a ball!" grins Brother Lindley.)

After his wife's death, Brother Lindley moved to Hobbs, New Mexico, where his father lived, to work in the oil field. Sister Frank Martin, the pastor's wife there, was the first to mention me to Brother Lindley, saying she hoped that we could "meet some time." And LaJoyce decided that he would make a good "Uncle Perry."

The Texico District Camp Meeting was in high gear in August of 1963 when LaJoyce called me one afternoon. I lived in Borger, Texas, an hour's drive away. "Are you coming to the camp meeting tonight?"

"Yes."

"Will you let me introduce you to a good friend of mine?"

A long pause. "Oh, I guess it won't hurt anything to meet him!"

I did dress with a bit more care that night, dashing on extra perfume. My brother and I arrived at intermission between youth service and night service. LaJoyce was watching and "managed" to walk in the direction of her "good friend," whom she had already asked to treat me to a coke (and he had agreed).

The evening was very warm, and after the proper introduction, he asked if I would like a coke before the evening service began. As we were making our way through the crowd, *another* young eligible widow stopped him and very near took up all his time asking questions and chattering on and on!

"Well," I said to myself, *"If I had not already promised him I'd go for a coke, I'd walk off and let her have him!"*

After the cold drink, I went to sit with my sister (Sister T. H. Chapman) who asked me, "Well, how did it go?"

"Aw. . . ," I replied, side-stepping the question. A few minutes later, he passed by trying to find a place to sit. I leaned over to her and whispered, "He *does* have pretty hair, doesn't he?"

"Watch out!" she remarked.

I fully intended to avoid him after the service, but my sister shamed me, so I asked her to go with me to find him and I would tell him I enjoyed meeting him. It was his last night to be there.

He took my comments as encouragement and asked for my address. This was my "undoing"! LaJoyce had made up her mind that if I did not "do something" about this one, she was going to mark my name off her Lonely Hearts list forevermore!

I watched the mail for several weeks, but no letter came. *"I guess he has no intentions of getting any better acquainted,"* I thought. *"Well, that's all right with me!"*

About a month later, however, he dropped by my home in Borger on his way to start a revival in Vernon, Texas. I was ironing, and since I wanted to get the ironing finished that Saturday afternoon, I just kept right on ironing and visiting, not realizing he had to be in Vernon *that* night.

"I just traded for another car." He seemed excited. I expected to see a nice, shiny car out front. But alas, when he escorted me to the car to eat out, it was a Volkswagen! My feathers fell! I am 5'7" tall and felt like the story I had read in school about the overgrown man riding a small donkey, his feet dragging the ground, and everyone asking him why he didn't get off and carry the donkey!

I jokingly tell people that Brother Lindley proposed to me on our first time out. What he actually said when he took me out to eat was: "If you don't want to marry a preacher, you had better run me off!"

"How do you do that tactfully?" I answered.

A few scattered letters from him found their way to my mail box, and I fear my return letters were not the most diplomatic of manuscripts. But soon I was watching *anxiously* for the mail and *praying* between letters that I had not said anything to offend him!

Then I had a *terrible* thought. Since he was twenty-nine years old before he married his former wife, maybe he had been married before! (I couldn't imagine anyone waiting *that* long to marry!) If he had, this would end it all for me. I wrote asking—and waited with apprehension for his answer, for by now I knew it would hurt. I was at last in love again. My fears were unfounded, my relief sweet.

On December 24, 1963, a beautiful Christmas Eve, we were married with all eleven of my brothers and sisters present. They all wanted to meet the man who had finally captured my heart.

After thirty years of widowhood, Brother Caughron's prediction came to pass: "You'll wind up marrying one!"

Happiness is never "never"!

Happiness is. . .

. . .a visit from an Archangel

By Glenda McGuire

"Glenda, will you sit by Bruce at the banquet?" my girlfriend asked.

As an eighth grader, the graduation banquet was near. Bruce, the class brain and artist—one of those top smart ones—was a little too shy to ask me.

"No!" I immediately replied, so shocked and shy that I gave it no consideration.

There was no afterthought except when my friends would come around and tell me I was crazy for not accepting. After all, he would buy my first corsage, too.

That was probably my first real contact with a possible date. Oh, once before, when I was younger, a close friend sent me a valentine saying, "Love and kisses to you from me. . .but I'd like to deliver them personally." I blushed and tucked the valentine away, not wanting anyone to see it. Shyness was my closest companion, a real problem to me.

After this approach, I began to receive eyes and admirations from several boys. Being raised in the church all my life, and being taught real consecration to God, I definitely would not consider dating anyone outside the church. It never entered my mind to look at sinner boys. My very thoughts, ambitions, and work was always around the church. My dad pastored in Arlington, Texas, for most of my growing-up years.

Suitors came and went. The first, a young man who moved to our city and attended our church, fell for me. I liked him and enjoyed his company, but often I preferred to go get cokes with the girls. He was disappointed, but persistent. After several years of dating, I still felt nothing serious for him. *"Surely there is something more for me,"* I thought.

A young evangelist came by. He was a college graduate and very intelligent. But he drove a *Volkswagon!* I was too embarrassed to go out with him. We did not drive big cars, but Volkswagons were not very popular then, and they made so much *noise!* I felt everyone could hear him coming.

Another preacher came along. I did not want anyone to know I cared anything for him, because he was not a good preacher. (Perhaps I should say he could not deliver a thought too well; he was inexperienced.)

Another evangelist looked my way. I just prayed,

"Lord, please don't make me fall in love with him. I don't want to marry him!" I had really set my ideas on someone who would not be a preacher. I loved going to church and working in the church, but I just wanted to be a good saint and have a happy family life.

I waited for quite some time. I felt that someday I would meet someone who would really be *special* to me. Several boys came by, entered my thoughts for awhile, but then passed on to someone else.

I busied myself in the church, working with the piano and organ, or spending time with the youth. We organized a youth trio consisting of one boy, Mike, and two girls, Phyllis and Cynthia. They were very good. We made a practice session at least once or twice a week for several hours. We attended all the youth rallies, meetings, and all other church activities. We drove many miles back and forth to singings. Those were very happy, carefree days.

"You have a secret admirer!" someone mentioned to me after several months. That was quite a shock! I just kept it to myself, not questioning it too much. *"There's always someone that blows things out of proportion,"* I thought. Someone was trying to start something new. My family and I, along with Mike and Phyllis, went to General Conference. I had no idea that Mike paid any attention to me!

"I decided then I was out to get your heart!" he told me later. However, time marched on and I did not know his plans.

"How about me coming over to your house and. . .you know. . .us sorta studying together?" Mike mentioned when school started again.

"Sure, that would be fine!" I said. So it became a

regular practice to study together two or three times a week. It was beginning to be clear that he had other motives in mind, which I sort of liked also.

Our first date was to a singing. He invited his sister to go along so that things would not look too obvious. We had a great time.

The next time, he invited me to go alone with him to a special singing out of town. He was careful not to ruin his plans, however. He did not come on too strong, just wanted to be "good friends." Since he did not have a steady girlfriend, and neither was I dating, we could just be together for company. He was really trying to impress me slowly. He was doing a good job of it, too, because I was looking forward every day to seeing him!

"Mike, I heard that Glenda ran off and got married," his supervisor told him one day when he got to work. Mike was immediately "sick." He could hardly wait to get off work that night to go by the church to see if I was there and learn what had happened. I talked with him after church.

Real friendly-like he asked, "Have you gotten married?"

I went along with the joke. Then he wanted to know if I was telling the truth. After some fun, I finally told him, "No."

Then we had a revival—with a single evangelist, no less. To my surprise, a dozen red roses were delivered to me. I did not know who really sent them. So I read the card, very shaky inside. It was signed "The Archangel" (Mike's name was *Michael*!). Did I ever get shook up! Red roses meant he loved me! Oh, I was in ecstasy! I felt I had really met the *special* one that I had been looking for.

We shared many good times together while dating. We had much in common; we both loved music and played instruments. Mike could tear up a bass, and was no slouch on the guitar. We spent many evenings at the piano, singing and talking.

On December 18, 1968, Mike asked me to marry him. Oh, what excitement! I really loved him. . .he was that *special* one I had searched a lifetime for. No one else made my heart beat so fast with the thrill of his presence. When I looked into those beautiful brown eyes and at that dark hair, I could hardly believe my good fortune. *"How could I ever have won the heart of one so handsome?"*

He bought me a stereo for Christmas, and on December 26, we became officially engaged by setting the wedding date for June 14, 1969. The next unforgettable six months were packed with plans for a great future together. We started looking for furniture and all that goes with starting a home.

"I got something today that I felt like we would need when we get married!" Mike was all excited.

"Oh, what?" I asked.

"A dog. And guess what I named it? *Lou!*" (That happened to be my middle name.) That brought a good laugh; the two doctors for whom I worked wrapped a big box of dog food and presented it to me as a wedding gift. But for some unknown reason, Lou expired before our wedding.

The wedding went beautifully, with more friends attending than I had anticipated. The bright pink and pastel pink made a pretty combination. I was walking on the clouds with my "Archangel, Michael." I finally got the man of my dreams—the *special* man.

A few days later, guess what he chose to tell me? "I feel like I may be called to preach." Can you imagine?

"Well, if you are not, I will be happy to be your wife, but if you are, I will go with you," was my response.

Now, fifteen years and two precious girls later, the pastor's wife in Gladewater, Texas, and wife of the Youth President of the Texas District, I am still in love with that *special* man I married—"The Archangel." He has sent me red roses many times since.

The Archangel's Bride, June 14, 1969.

Happiness is. . .

*. . .a long distance
telephone call*

By LaJoyce Martin

"I didn't have a chance! You went to a Higher Power!" said my husband. And that's just what I did!

We never had a date. I prayed for Elroy Martin for *five* years!

Over six feet tall, freckle-faced, and (let's face it) no beauty queen, what hope did I have with this good looking, dedicated, blue-eyed hunk of masculinity two thousand miles away?

Competition for single preachers was fierce then as now. One young lady resorted to tucking an onion in her handkerchief so she could "weep" at the altar, leaving the

203

impression she was spiritual. Yet another requested herself to sing, so as to traipse right in front of him on her way to the platform! I just put callouses on my knees.

Ironically, my husband and I were born in the same small community of Walnut Springs, Texas, a block apart, a year apart. Romantically, our birth certificates shared the same file cabinet in the Bosque County Courthouse! (Can't you see my birth certificate winking at his all the way across the alphabet from the B's to the M's?)

His father, Reverend Frank Martin, pastored my parents, the Donald Berrys, when I was born. But alas, before I was a year old our ways parted.

Only sporadically over the years did our paths cross. I remember every one of them; he remembers almost none of them!

"I just feel like I'm going to marry Elroy Martin, and there's not a thing I can do about it!" I told Mom when I was seventeen years old. Just graduated from Plainview High School, he came with his dad to help on our new church building project in Cleburne, Texas, that year. My heart did flipflops!

"I think the Lord is dealing with him to preach," I heard his mother say, but as yet he had not acknowledged that call. It was not the glamor of marrying a young evangelist that infatuated me; I fell in love with the *man*. But he paid no attention whatsoever to me, and I certainly solicited none. It was as if I did not exist!

Fortunately, my younger brother Bobby established a friendship with Elroy. I kept Bobby corresponding with him over the weeks that followed with all sorts of bribes! I even helped compose Bobby's humorous letters. But space between them grew wider and wider.

Months passed. The Martin family moved to New Mexico. Mom joined my prayer force; I was graduated from high school and needed some answers. Dad had a square underground prayer room beneath his study; the trap door to it was concealed by a shaggy throw rug. I borrowed this damp, musty prayer square for a talk with the Lord.

"Now Lord," I prayed, never more sincere, "I want to know *for sure* that Elroy Martin is the man I'm supposed to marry. If he is, then get him to our District Conference in Dallas this week."

It was a big order. Elroy said he had not *planned* to be there at all. He was en route back to New Mexico from a revival! Dallas was out of his way. But a minister friend insisted on the stop, and Elroy delayed catching his bus until the following day. Dad (bless him!) offered him a ride back as far as Cleburne, several miles closer to his destination, and a night's lodging. Bobby inconspicuously seated Elroy in the back seat with me, and I almost died of heart-palpitations! But he still did not seem to be aware that I was on planet earth.

We girls had a crazy game going the year I finished school. Merely kid-stuff, it resulted in many a good laugh. We counted one hundred red convertibles, then located a woman wearing an orchid-colored suit, followed in sequence by a man wearing a solid green necktie. The next guy we saw would be our groom!

It took awhile to fill that prescription, but by the summer of 1955, I was down to the tie. I found it! It was bright green and entwined about a preacher's neck at the Texico District Conference in Abilene. Sitting beside him was Elroy Martin!

Then, horror of horrors! When I was nineteen, I heard that my heartthrob was engaged to be married that fall, 1956. My faith was sorely tried! I prayed with such anguish that I am sure God used my tears to dissolve his wedding plans.

My "Jonah" then took off for a far country, California, where I "lost" him for some two years. I began dating some of the local church boys off and on during that interim. The enemy would have me settle for an Ishmael, and after dating steadily for about a year, decision time came. "A bird in the hand is worth two in the bush," the carnal side of me said, for I surely did not want to be an old maid! It must be remembered Elroy Martin had shown me no personal attention—by letter, phone, or in person. And I was not getting any younger!

Back to the prayer square. When I came in one night, having promised the young man I was dating and myself that I would come to some conclusion about my future, I pulled a promise from my well-used promise box. The words jumped out at me: "*WAIT,* I say, on the Lord. . . ." Had God spoken aloud, it could not have been more definite.

A holy boldness seized me; I had nothing to lose. Elroy's twenty-second birthday was approaching, and I decided to send him a birthday card. I did not even know his address; I heard that he was Brother David Gray's assistant pastor in San Diego. I sent the card in care of Brother Gray. The comic card went something like this: "Almost missed your birthday. . .The thought makes me squirm. . .In fact, to put it truthfully. . .I feel just like this worm!" (Open the card and out pops a spring, painted like a worm.) I penned in, "Hey, man, you're gettin' old!" And signed my name. It was April of 1958.

God had already started working on the California side of the border. Bernard Elms, a cousin of Elroy's, had just lost his girl friend and was having withdrawals. When Elroy got my card, he went to Bernard. "Say, I got a card today from this girl back in Texas. . . ." He proceeded to tell Bernard every nice thing about me that he could remember.

Nonchalantly, Bernard answered, "That all sounds fine, but she's two thousand miles from here!" and dropped the subject.

Back in his tiny bachelor's apartment, Elroy began to think—or the Lord began to talk. "Now if that girl back in Texas is everything I told Bernard she is, then why not like her myself?" he asked himself, not realizing his thinking was being colored by some stiff prayers eastward. He sat down and wrote me a friendly letter before that week was out.

Quote from that first letter, April 8, 1958: "Well, if you are not writing or keeping company with any young man I would like to make this the beginning of a conversation by communication. If you are actively engaged with any one else, I will not accept a second to the motion."

One small personal commitment saved my life! Our church was in revival, and I made it a policy not to date anyone during revivals.

"I want to stay and pray in the altar after church as long as I wish, without worrying about some guy waiting around to take me for a Coke!" I told my friends. "There'll be no dating until the revival ends." I broke all ties, curtailed all social life, and put my whole self into the services.

The letter from Elroy arrived one day before the revival closed. . .I could honestly say I was dating no one.

207

Again, God's timing was perfect!

My head was in the clouds! A few letters later, he wrote, "Don't get any too big ideas about me." Get any? Why, I'd had 'em for four years!

Then on June 23, the day of Mom and Dad's Silver Anniversary, he abruptly broke off the correspondence. The despair I felt showed up on the pages of my diary.

Monday, June 23, 1958: "I got the long-awaited letter from Elroy, but it was a FAREWELL—says he doesn't think we were made for each other. I practically had a spasm. Cried and bawled and squawled. . .To no avail. He's gone. . . ."

Excerpt from "The Story of Our Engagement" in'wedding book: "I resolved to wait two weeks in fasting and prayer and if nothing farther developed, to crush the rose forever, and replant an uprooted heart in a garden elsewhere."

Cornelius' prayers could not hold a light to mine! Every morning when the Lord got up, the first thing He saw was a great hump in heaven's floor where my prayers were pushing up through the clouds!

On Friday, June 27, my faith was recovering. The diary says "I am, in the back of my mind, expecting Elroy to call. . . ." And that was the day it happened!

I think I knew when the telephone rang late that afternoon that it was he. Dad must have suspected it too; he got on the extension phone! While Elroy was proposing, Dad was writing as fast as the pencil would move, trying to get it all down in black and white.

That illegal document, now in my possession, is numbered from one to twenty-four. There are twenty-three "he-saids" and one "she-said." That was No. 17. Most of the sentences are maddeningly incomplete, but here's a sampling:

2. I decided. . .there's nobody but you.

11. I always. . .

14. I can talk this out with Brother Gray.

16. Would you. . .have me as your husband. . . .

17. O.K. (LaJoyce)

18. You. . . .

20. . . .I'm real happy, how about you?

21. We get together on something soon.

23. I want to. . . .

24. I really love you. Bye. (Last words.)

When I hung up the phone, I was engaged to be married to the man of my dreams! I was so excited that I actually remembered very little of the conversation!

Diary entry, Saturday, June 28, 1958: "This day I can do little more than daydream. Mom is trying to teach me to make tea. . .I am drying dishes, putting them in quaint and queer places. I am very, very happy today. I feel that God's will is definitely being worked out. Oh, praise the Lord! My heart has been singing praises to the Lord all day."

Written in the back of the 1958 diary: "Years end terribly often. . . . Yet, I marvel how so short a period of time can be packed with such changes as my life has experienced the past 365 days. Little did I dare to dream at the onset of 1958 that by its curtain closing, I would be engaged to the man of my dreams, and of the deep pleasure of planning, thinking, hoping that would be mine. I believe I've shed more tears, yet had more triumph than any other year of my earthly existence."

"Did I get a letter today, Mom?" (My daily question.)

During our eleven-month-engagement, he wrote me a letter almost every day. He did not have money for phone calls. He returned from California only once, riding the bus for three days and three nights to reach the Amarillo Camp Meeting before I left on Saturday morning. I got to see him there for less than one hour! Of that semi-hour, the diary says: "We talked a bit, it seems so short and vague, but he was there, smiling and standing near me. . . ."

Bobby drove me four hundred miles to New Mexico to hear him preach one night, and Elroy made the return trip with us, leaving the next day for New Mexico and his return flight to California. As he departed, he tossed his handkerchief out the window to me. Now I had something tangible! A dirty handkerchief! I still have it.

When Elroy discussed his plans for marriage with his superior, Brother Gray told him frankly: "You are breaking every rule I have, but I *feel like* you are doing the right thing." Yet another victory, as Elroy would never have overstepped his pastor's advice.

The lovely saints at San Diego gave Elroy a wedding shower. They made his "bride" out of a mop, using the mopstrings for hair, and fashioning a pink poster-board face for "her." This, they insisted, he keep with him at all times during the evening's activities.

Some of our love letters, inadvertently stored under a faulty hot water heater, were destroyed by water. In March of 1959, he wrote asking how soon I could be ready after May 1 for the wedding. My reply, dated March 23, says: "As far as I'm concerned, it could be fifteen minutes past midnight of May 1st!"

He arrived on Saturday, May 16, 1959, at 6:30 p.m., forgetting that he was scheduled to preach in Hillsboro, thirty miles away, that night. Brother N. J. Jones, who had printed our wedding invitations without charge, took up our first offering. Elroy gave me the pennies. Those six copper-colored wheat coins now live in my wedding book.

We were married six days later, on Friday, May 22. The six days were spent scurrying about in preparation. I bought the marriage license!

The wedding was every ounce as wild as the courtship! Tornado clouds moved in near town and the electricity went off in the northern section of the city as the hour of our union neared. We delayed the starting time a half hour, waiting for the attendants to get through the storm. Approximately 150 guests braved the fierce weather to witness my miracle, but two groomsmen did not show up at all. My choice of soft rainbow colors clashed with the elements and won.

The ceremony was scheduled for 8:00 p.m.; it began raining at 7:00—a deluge. The lawn, designated for our reception, was an inch underwater. I pulled off my white shoes, gathered my long wedding dress (that hid my calloused knees!) about me, and waded water to the church from the parsonage.

Elroy wrote our vows himself. I can hear him saying it now, "I wanted to be sure to get all the 'obeys' in!" His dad married us, and I sailed through the "I do's" and "I will's" admirably, then dropped my bride's bouquet right in front of everybody! Not waiting for my matron of honor to retrieve it, I made one grand swoop and picked it up from the floor myself.

We moved the "lawn reception" into the auditorium, the only available place for it. A large miller bug dived with glee into the punch and swam the full length of the bowl!

Most brides would have been in a frenzy of tears by this time; but not I! I had waited *five* years for this moment, shed enough tears for a lifetime, and no amount of tribulation could mar my newfound happiness! I smiled all the way through!

We had been given $35 cash for our honeymoon, but the Lord had taken care of that, too. A family friend, a proprietor of a motel-restaurant in Hooks, Texas, near Texarkana promised, "When you two get married, I'll give you my best room." The food from her grill was "on the house."

On Sunday, we attended church in Texarkana where a revival was in progress. Pastor Shearer asked us to sing; we had never sung a duet before! Our first song was "Nothing Can Compare," and our second, "It Was a Miracle." We attended services every night thereafter of our honeymoon, and on the last night, my new husband gave us away by saying, "Now this sounds strange to me, because I've never said it before, but I'd like for my *wife* to testify." The light dawned on the audience.

The magnolia trees were in magnificent bloom in East Texas. Brother Shearer loaned us his boat and we went fishing on Lake Texarkana, picked wild plums, and painted "Tom Sawyer" and "Becky Thatcher" on our straw hats. Ceramics of Tom and Becky sit on our piano today.

In my wedding book, I wrote: "Dear God, grant that our precious rose always continue to flourish in Love's Garden with YOU as Gardener."

And that prayer has been answered. In 1984, we celebrated our Silver Wedding Anniversary and now we're going for Gold—whether it be May 22, 2009 A.D. or in heaven!

This is the picture that sat on my bureau for five years, bringing hope and cheer.

The day "I chased him for five years," I told a friend "and he finally caught me!"

Leaving town for honeymoon.

What? No letter?

"Dear Lord, I ask nothing for myself, but please send my mother a son-in-law."

Tom Sawyer and Becky Thatcher

Happiness is. . .

. . .being expelled from school with him.

By Mary Ann Mayville

"Hey, little lady, what are you gonna be when you grow up?" asked Daddy, as he crossed his legs, sat me on his foot, and began to swing me.

Looking up into his face with the dreamy look of a five-year-old, I said, "I'm gonna be a housewife and the best mother there is!" Even then, down inside, I knew I was going to marry a preacher. How or when was another matter!

We lived in Spicewood, Texas, a ranching community with one store and post office. The church we attended in Johnson City was a distance of thirty-five miles one way,

217

and the only boys there were my brothers.

There were nine boys and two girls in my family. Mama's motto was: "Babies are my business." Things were usually quite lively around our house!

My sister, Marsalyn, and the four older boys had already left home when Daddy decided to make different arrangements as to our schooling. He decided that the nearest town, Marble Falls, fifteen miles away, did not have the "small town atmosphere" he desired for us. So Mama taught us at home for a year.

In 1974, the next year, Daddy enrolled us in a private A.C.E. school in Kingsland, Texas. The church sponsoring the school did not hold to our doctrinal teachings.

I was sixteen years old when Daddy enrolled us in the private school, and I had given little thought to marriage. Besides, what boy in his right mind would drive fifty miles one way to see me—and be converged upon by five lively brothers who thought it their duty to inspect each and every detail of a newcomer. Was his nose long? Did he have a Northern accent?

I was totally unprepared for what met my eyes that second day at the A.C.E. school. Classes were in progress at mid-morning when the door opened abruptly. In stepped the most handsome young man I had ever seen! I thought my heart was going to race away!

He was of medium heighth, blonde, slender, yet stocky. He held a Bible in his right hand and wore a long trench coat which billowed out behind as he strode purposefully into the room. The sunlight beamed on his golden hair and caught there. It was dazzling! Except for a slight nod and a brief smile, he hardly noticed me.

I was from a strong Oneness Pentecostal home,

where the Scriptures were drilled into our minds thoroughly. Suddenly, the desire to win that young man to the truth became my foremost thought and prayer.

I found out more about him. He was the "Randy" everyone had been talking about. He lived nearby on a youth ranch. The Little Israel Christian Ranch sent about fifteen students to our school. They had been in a revival in Louisiana, and Randy was a little late coming to school.

"Hey, Mary," Tim said on the way home, "Did you see the new guy?"

"Did I see the new guy? How do you forget such blue eyes?" I thought.

I witnessed to Randy, and Randy tried to witness to me, but God had His way and on February 12, 1975, Randy was baptized in Jesus' name!

When the school principal found out that Randy was one of those United Pentecostals, he thought it best to expel both of us before anyone else became contaminated with this Jesus name message. Thank the Lord, I got him first!

By this time, we were serious about each other. My dream of "that preacher someday" had come true.

In August, at my brother Gregory's wedding, I caught the bouquet of my sister-in-law, LaKay. "Oh, Randy!" I squealed, but Randy was nowhere to be seen. The back door offered an easy escape for his red face!

We were both seventeen at this time. Six days after Gregory married, we decided to seek earnestly for God's direction for our lives. We found a secluded (we thought) dirt road on which to have a prayer meeting.

The Holy Ghost filled the little Subaru and we felt His assurance. But our joy was not shared by the people who drove up beside us quite unexpectedly and rolled down their window. Seeing Randy's worried look, and the tears on my face, they demanded, "What do you think you're doing?"

"We're just praying," I answered, making a feeble attempt at a smile. Their looks of astonishment said it louder than words, "A likely story!"

They informed us that we were on private property. We apologized nervously and headed back to town. Halfway there, Randy pulled the car over and said, "Just to be formal, will you marry me?" (One problem with economy cars is that there isn't enough room to shout!)

"Oh, yes, Honey, I will!"

Saturday, October 25, was rehearsal night. We were on our way to pick up the archway and candles when I heard an excited, "Oh, Jesus! Oh, Jesus!" Randy was pulling me down. The next instant we crashed into the back of a car in front of us that had come to a complete stop on the bridge; our brakes had failed on the wet pavement! When I was finally able to get up, all I could see was muddy water. Our car came to rest on the railing of the bridge.

"What now, Lord?" I thought. The car was totaled!

At the ceremony, Randy could not kneel without grimacing. Or was he praying, *"God help us now; we're going to need it"*?

We were without the benefit of a car, but Marsalyn, my sister, and her little girl agreed to take us wherever we wanted to go. Flat broke, our motel turned out to be the church evangelistic quarters.

Four days later found us in Sealy, Texas, harvesting pecans for Brother Shelton Fluitt. We arrived at twelve midnight and all the motels in town were full, so Randy put a mattress in the back of Gregory's Datsun pickup. At least it had a camper shell! What a honeymoon!

"Pssssst. Randy, what's that?" I asked in the quietest whisper possible. There it was again! "Randy, wake up! Did you hear that?" Immediately, he was wide awake.

The fog had rolled in with zero visibility. Several coyotes decided to pay us a visit! I was so scared that all I could do was pray! The Lord protected us, however, because we woke up alive in the morning.

Not wishing to repeat that experience, we moved into the old farmhouse. It was built on stilts. Two rooms were used to store pecans, and we slept in the dining room. With one small electric heater and a mountain of blankets, we survived the coldest winter ever.

Hearing a commotion in the pecan room one night, Randy grabbed on a pair of baggy overalls. With the only weapon he could find—a scoop shovel—he cautiously opened the door a tiny crack. Since it was about two o'clock in the morning, I held the flashlight for him. Of all the holloring! Our intruder turned out to be a rat, approximately a foot and a half in length, who had come to feast on pecans. Each time Randy slammed his huge shovel down, his feet came several inches off the floor.

"Watch out, here he comes!" I screamed in terror. The poor rat finally escaped through a hole. We collapsed on the floor laughing at ourselves.

In February of 1976, we moved back to Johnson City, finding a small one-bedroom house. Randa Michelle made her appearance on October 8, 1976, and we became three. Krystal Estelle joined us on January 5, 1978, and in June, the Lord blessed us with our first real home—and my dream to be the best housewife and mother became a reality. Randy assisted Sister Fluitt at Johnson City and evangelized on weekends.

We had just accepted God's call to home missions a few days before our home burned and we lost everything on February 12, 1981. Yet another daughter Keli Faith, blessed our home on October 29, of that year, making a total of three beautiful, blue-eyed, blonde-haired girls.

We are still pastoring Daystar United Pentecostal Church in Georgetown, Texas. October 27, 1985, will mark ten years of happiness and love.

Mrs. Mary Ann *Mayville*—what a beautiful name!

Happiness is. . .

. . .a wink by the watertower

By Sandra Myer

The day was tense with excitement. Months of preparation had gone into this day. Preachers and laity all across the Texas District had gathered for the motorcade to the groundbreaking of Texas Bible College.

This was a new venture by the Texas District, and everyone was enthused over the opportunities to produce quality men and women for the Lord's work. The officials were all misty-eyed as they realized their prayers and dreams actually were now going to be a reality.

Somewhere in that large enthusiastic group was a fourteen-year-old girl and her mother. This young teenage girl turned to her mother and said, "Mother, just think, I'm going to marry a man that will come to this Bible college."

I don't really know if that statement was prophecy, faith or just a young girl's dream, but some twenty-one years later I remember making that statement.

At about twelve I started a nightly ritual in my prayer. "Lord," I would pray, "Let me marry a man that is consecrated to You; let him be a good daddy to our kids and let him love me. Lord, I'd like for him to be handsome but that doesn't matter nearly as much as all the rest." I guess I felt that I shouldn't ask God for too much.

God, being omnipresent, was working on a seventeen-year-old boy fifteen hundred miles away in the little town of Vista, California. Struggling with the will of God in his life, he prayed much about his future during his senior year of high school. Bible college was still just a dream in his youthful heart.

Upon the recommendation of his pastor, Brother Johnny Hodges, he was offered a scholarship by the president of Western Apostolic Bible College. This was a golden opportunity to attend a great school; however, the closer it got to registration day, the more he felt that this open door was not the perfect will of God for him. A very strong desire to attend the new Bible college in Texas tugged at his mind and heart.

Two weeks before he was to leave for Western Apostolic Bible College, he sold his car and secured enough money to get to Houston and pay down on his tuition at Texas Bible College. God was working to put legs on a young girl's faith in prayer.

The fall of 1966 I started my senior year in high

school. Many of my friends at school were already engaged and some were even married. I felt like an old maid for sure since I didn't even have a steady beau at that time. Oh, there were dates scattered here and there but many Friday nights were spent in my room questioning and praying, "When Lord?"

Our youth leader, Brother Nelson Neyland, came to me on one occasion: "Sandra, the Bible says if you'll be faithful over little, God will make you ruler over much. Stay faithful, God has a special plan for you." With that encouragement I stayed faithful, even to giving up my Sunday afternoon nap to go to a street meeting the youth leader had planned. Although I had always considered it of utmost ignorance to have street meetings, when it was announced for the next Sunday, I made a commitment to participate. My only consolation was that since I would be playing the accordian I could sit and hide among the group as they were standing.

I walked into my Sunday school class on Sunday morning; I was introduced to the speaker for the street meeting. "Sandra, this is David Myer from Texas Bible College. He will be preaching this afternoon at the street meeting," a friend remarked. I thought to myself, *"H-m-m-m, this street meeting might not be so bad after all."* Sunday afternoon found me on Congress Avenue in downtown Houston, seated and hid with my accordian but with a beeline view of the preacher.

There was one converted to the Lord from that street meeting and one converted to David Myer (needless to say who that was). After he had preached and perspired until he didn't have a dry thread on, he looked at me and I melted. We stood there and talked until everyone else had left and my ride was sitting at the curb blowing the horn intensely. Finally I came out of my fog to realize I did need a ride home, so I bid him goodbye.

On that Sunday night, Brother O. R. Fauss, my pastor, invited the young preacher to stay and be the evening speaker. He preached, "What Does God Really Hate?" I was thinking *"Who does David Myer really love?"*

Our organist, upon seeing the stars in my eyes, offered to let me play the invitation at the close of his message. I was awe struck. I felt like *the evangelist's wife* as I made my way to the organ that night.

Flipping to the index of the songbook, I decided to play "Sin Can Never Enter There." As I played ever so carefully, the evangelist's voice boomed, "As a song of invitation is sung, we open these altars." Oh! I hadn't bargained for that. I felt safe playing, but singing a solo petrified me.

With no time to delay, however, I started, "Sin can never enter there," but my alto voice had a terrible time adjusting to the key the song was written in. I was humiliated and embarrassed! No preacher would ever want a wife that sang like that even if she had curly eyelashes.

After church that night he asked me for my phone number which I gladly gave to him. The next day I came in from school and Daddy casually remarked, "Some boy called for you today but I told him you were at school."

"Who was it?" I excitedly asked. "Was it David Myer?"

"Seems like he said his name was David *Somebody.* I'm not sure, but he acted surprised that you were still young enough to be in high school," replied Daddy.

"Oh Daddy, he'll think I'm a kid! Why did you tell him I was still in school? Oh, he'll never call back again," I sobbed.

But he did call back again. . .and again. . .and again. Finally he asked me for that first big date. I thought he never would, but I didn't realize what all was involved when a Bible school student had a date. The Bible school rule was this: One date a month with a married chaperone along. This meant the student had to pay his date's way and the chaperone's way to wherever they went. On the meager salary of an after-school job, dates were few and far between. There were a few *illegal* dates that the dean would turn his head about, however, and our first date was one of those.

Our second date was *legal* with Glenn and Neil Seaman (a newly-wed couple) as our chaperons. We drove to Galveston Island and had a seafood dinner at the Golden Greek Restaurant. It took most of his paycheck for that date, and I'm sure he felt a little sick seeing how much food I left on my plate. (I was much too nervous to eat.) Many times after that, our dates consisted of driving to the high school where he worked, washing blackboards together and sharing a sack lunch my mother would kindly pack for us.

It was during this time that I did much soul searching and praying. I felt that the perfect will of God was very important in my life; and then the phone calls quit coming. "Oh, no," I thought, "should I have prayed so hard for the *perfect* will of God?"

I graduated from high school in June of 1967 and began packing for the Texas youth camp. After several days at youth camp, I was walking down the sidewalk past the old water tower when suddenly my eyes looked up into a most familiar face. One eye winked as I gasped,

"Uh. . .David. . .h-h-hi!"

A smile crept over his face as he returned my greeting.

I literally ran back to the cabin where I was staying, tore my brand new dress on the old screen door, flung myself across the bed and cried, "Oh, he'll think I'm so forward! I didn't mean to wink at him! He'll surely not like me now!"

I berated myself until I saw him again a week later at the Texas campmeeting. He seemed especially friendly and invited my sisters and me to sing at his upcoming revival in Liberty, Texas.

We practiced our trio, curled our eyelashes and headed for the revival meeting. Upon entering the church that night, I was greeted by a young lady who introduced herself and explained that she had been invited by the evangelist to the revival to sing. My eyelashes drooped and my throat went dry. She asked me if I would mind playing the piano for her solo. So I played for her solo, played for our trio, and then prayed for God's will to be done.

Long distance calls started coming at a frequent rate again after that night in Liberty, and the mailman started delivering more mail to the Bridges' residence. Plans were made to spend Labor Day together. As we visited together on that Labor Day, we both realized what we wanted in a companion; although there were other opportunities presented to each of us at that time, God was guiding us together.

Our conversation turned to our future many times in the next couple of weeks, but *the question* had not officially been asked. On September 18, he called me at work and suggested we drive to Galveston that evening. "Why, certainly, I'd love to go!" I replied excitedly, remembering that was where our first *legal* date had been to and thinking about the romantic atmosphere that prevailed there. I hurried home from work to get beautified by 7:00 p.m.

When he arrived at the door that evening, he looked a little pale and seemed especially quiet. I tried to keep chatter flowing for the fifty-mile drive to the island, but that strange silence still prevailed. We parked the car, walked out on the fishing pier and watched the waves as they crashed against the rocks in the moonlight. It was a beautiful night, the stars were shining, and the sound of the water provided a perfect backdrop for him to pop *the question;* but. . .we walked hand in hand silently back to the car.

We pulled back on to the boulevard and mixed in with the flow of traffic heading back to Houston. After what seemed an eternity of silence, David turned to me and with trembling voice said, "Sandra, will you marry me?"

"Oh yes," I replied quicker than I intended to. "Oh yes!" That tender moment was shattered by the sound of a burglar alarm going off in a nearby building, and we both suddenly began to laugh. We had been to one of the most romantic spots in the state of Texas all evening and now, in the midst of traffic and sirens, we were making our plans to be married.

We stopped back by Glenn and Neil Seaman's apartment to tell them the news. There, we got out the calendar and decided on December 15, 1967, to be our wedding date. We stopped by to tell my sister Doris and her husband and then we went on home to share the news with Mother and Daddy.

I, being the baby of the family, had already witnessed Mother's tears each time my three sisters had come in with their announcement and I worried about how it would affect her. As we walked into the living room that night, she must have seen the pure joy in both of us because instead of tears there was great joy at our announcement. Daddy was already asleep so we decided not to disturb him. It comes to mind, now some seventeen years later that David never did ask him for my hand in marriage; however, he's one of Daddy's favorite sons-in-law, so I guess it was all right.

Wedding plans started being made, and for the next three months florists, dressmakers and caterers took up every spare minute. Revivals kept the groom-to-be out of town most of the time during that engagement period, so all the details were left to the bride. I counted it all joy, however, to make the preparations to become Mrs. David Myer. I began to cross the days off my calendar. Some time it seemed like I didn't have enough time left and then at other times it seemed as though December 15 would never arrive.

I shall never forget the last Sunday night service before our wedding on Friday night. I went to service realizing that I was leaving the security of my home church that I had been a part of since birth. I was marrying an evangelist and would be in a different church every two to three weeks. How would this affect me spiritually? I would be leaving my pastor, my family, my friends, my home; it was scary. I cried through most of the service and then that calm assurance flooded my soul. I realized I was going in God's perfect will and that it was He who had made all these things meaningful to me anyway. He would go with me.

Friday, December 15, 1967, at 8:00 p.m., the organ music was softly playing, the candles were flickering, the bridesmaid's were standing gracefully in a row, the groomsmen were all standing stiffly in their tuxedos, the flower girl and miniature bride and groom were wiggling, the preachers had their little black book and *I* was the Bride.

I looked down the long aisle and quickly saw the handsome face of the one I love, the one I pledged my life to, the one my children will call Dad, the one I will get angry with, the one I will make up with, the one I will share sorrow with, the one I will share joy with, the one I will grow old with. I took a deep breath, put my arm through my Dad's and whispered, "I'm ready."

Happiness is. . .

. . .sneaking a look at his picture

By Dolores Neely

"Oh, Daddy, you can't mean we are moving?" I wailed.

"It looks that way," he said in that soft, low voice which he never raised to any of his three daughters. Jack Van Winkle was a company man, and if Humble Oil Company said "Move!" he moved. Somehow I think he had a little adventurous blood in him. This move was a good promotion for him, and his family should have been very happy.

Settling down in the New London, Texas, community was soon accomplished, and the rest of the summer dragged on. Then it came time to register for enrollment at Kilgore Junior College. After a long, dull summer I was happy to meet new people and make friends. One girl with whom I became instant friends, was a girl who was United Pentecostal—Velma Neely.

Velma was a beautiful girl with dark hair, gray eyes, and a radiant smile which revealed perfect white teeth. Velma had two sisters, one just younger than she, named Rose Yvonne, and one eight years younger named Sandra. An older brother in the Air Force was due home in February. I saw his picture and thought surely that must be the most handsome man God had ever made.

I looked at that picture every time I visited in Velma's home, but resigned myself to the fact that he would never look my way. My mother had told me one time that I was going to find someone that would break my heart and sure enough I had found him! I thought, "If a little old picture would make me feel that way, what on earth would I do if I ever did get to behold him."

There was a Christ Ambassador Rally at my church in Carlisle on Monday night and I asked Velma to go with me. She told me to pick her up and she would go. She had also told me her brother had come in from Germany with his discharge from the United States Air Force.

"Velma, I am not coming in your house, so when you see me drive up, you come out to meet me. I am not going to let your brother think I can't wait to meet him and am coming in just to see him," I stated.

"Oh, silly, he will be gone tonight when you get to my house. He will be visiting some old buddies." She sounded so convincingly that I believed her.

February nights in East Texas can be very cold and it was just such a night when I went to the Neely's home for Velma. Since her brother was not to be home, I had consented to come in the house. She answered my knock and I stepped through the door. There I stood in my hunter green coat that hung from my shoulders to my ankles. When I finally got my eyes focused and looked across the room, I saw the most handsome man I had ever seen in my life. His mother was sitting beside him looking at his high school annual. She was every bit as beautiful as her son. She had black hair, beautiful gray eyes and the same gorgeous smile.

Very matter-of-factly Velma said, "Dolores, I would like you to meet my brother, Vernon."

I think I smiled, turned red, ducked my head and mumbled, "I am happy to meet you."

There is no schooling of life that could have prepared me for what I felt that cold wintry night. His hair was blond and wavey. His eyes were a dancing blue-gray, with enough mischief to see my discomfort. His flashing smile was the final blow which swept me away in the mighty swirl of emotions from which there is no rescue.

"Velma, why did you do that to me?" I struggled to say when we were in the car, and she knew I was shaken.

"Now, Dolores, don't feel bad. I really did think he would be gone, and anyway you needed to meet Vernon. He was glad to meet you," she said in her dry tone of voice.

On the bus to college the next morning we chatted about non-essentials until Velma asked me, "How much do you weigh?"

"How much do I weigh? What on earth do you want to. . . ?" I stopped in mid sentence. "Oh, no you don't. Who wants to know?" I remembered the big coat I had on the night before. It had hung just above my ankles and all Vernon Neely could see of me was my head, hands, ankles, and feet. "Well, you can just go home and tell your brother, too much."

That afternoon as I came up to catch the bus home, I could not believe my eyes. There was Vernon Neely surrounded by girls. I knew it would be like that, but I just never wanted to see it. If I did not see him with all the beautiful girls, I could still dream. He looked over one of the girl's head and smiled at me. I looked around to see at whom he was smiling. As I was about to step onto the bus, Velma called, "Wait a minute." I stood to the side and waited for her to come up to me.

"Come ride with me in Vernon's car," she said with a little more excitement than usual.

"I don't think so, Velma, there will be a full car as it is."

"Oh, silly, Vernon said for you to come." She grabbed my hand and pulled me toward the car. The door was open and she pushed me into the back seat, where there were no doors to open and get out. I thought I might as well make the best of it as the college beauty got in beside Vernon and talked in that deep drippy sweet voice. If I could ever get home, I wasn't going to pull this little trick again. It is just too hard on a body.

I sat looking out the window wondering how a man made you tongue-tied, pushing you into the depths of despair and to the heights of happiness all at the same time. When I looked toward the front of the car, I saw those beautiful mischievous eyes looking at me. All of a sudden it had turned very warm; I could not look into those eyes very long. His eyes were gray today, just like his mother's.

The next day, a boy named Joe asked me for a date

and told me we would be going with his neighbor and his date. Lo, it was Vernon Neely and a girl named Jo. Everywhere I turned, Vernon popped up. "Maybe it won't be so bad since we have dates," I thought.

When we got to the restaurant, we sat across the table from each other. I could not take my eyes off him, and sometimes I caught him looking at me. Sweet agony. Torture with invisible chains. After dinner, we left the restaurant and Joe and I walked awhile and talked. He asked me, "You have fallen in love with him, haven't you?"

I thought about this a while and said, "Yeah, I guess I have and I really don't know him." I think Joe even felt sorry for me that night.

I had been engaged to a sailor stationed on the west coast for about a year. We both knew the other was dating, but we neither one minded. We were just friends hoping for love. He was stationed at San Diego, California, and I never wanted to go to California. If he had been on a ship off the east coast, I probably would have married him just to go to that part of the United States. That would have been the most foolish mistake of my life.

My mother had told me one Saturday morning, after we had moved to New London, "Get in that bedroom and pray through over that Navy boy and the Lord will give you someone in the church, full of the Holy Ghost." I went to my bedroom; but I did not want to pray. Finally, I got down by my bed; I said a few words; I got up. I wrestled with what I knew I had to do until the time came when I really did pray and commit my life to God. There is nothing so sweet as victory in Jesus. He made me look at my life anew and know there had to be something more than friendship in my marriage; there had to be Love. I broke the engagement.

The next week of school, Vernon came often for us to ride home with him. There were always the beauties to vie for his attention and the middle of the front seat. On Friday, he took everyone else home first, and my heart so jumped around in my chest that I could hardly answer the questions he asked. I could not remember being this shy before. I really think he enjoyed my plight. I was expressing my thanks for the ride home when he stopped me: "Will you go with me tomorrow night?"

Would I go with him? I thought, honey, I'd go to the back side of the moon with you. I'd go to Africa, Alaska, anywhere, you just name it! Then I said, "I would love to. What time will you be here?"

Twenty-six hours can be a long time to wait when the most exciting moments of your life are about to happen. It can also be the shortest and most tortuous when you don't feel you are quite ready. I felt both.

Saturday night and seven o'clock came. I heard Vernon's car turn the corner. He stopped at our door and stepped out of his car, started up the walk, climbed the steps and knocked on the door. I knew in my heart there was no turning back from this moment on. I had found love. What I was going to do about it, I did not know. One thing was certain, I was going to talk to God. Vernon Neely did not have the Holy Ghost.

He stood in our door, so handsome, flashing that dazzling smile. My heart turned over. I invited him in to meet my family.

"Vernon, I would like you to meet my mother, my sister Mollie, and my baby sister Lela Jane. Oh yes, here are my nephew and niece, David and Debbie."

My dad was not home that night as he had to work late—which was usual. He was on twenty-four hour call at all times. I could hardly wait for these two special men to meet. My daddy was extremely perceptive where the character of a person was concerned.

The weather had warmed, the night was clear, and the stars were shining brightly. It was a perfect evening for a girl in love. Vernon helped me into his car. After he was seated behind the wheel, he turned to me, "Would you mind going to a store with me so I can buy a couple of shirts? I went to Tyler today, but I need a couple more shirts."

I had never gone to shop with a man before and really didn't know what to do or what was expected of me. I was excited, though, that he would want me to go with him.

When we got to Overton, he parked the car in front of Moses' Department Store and we went in. I was thankful there were just a few people in the store. The owner came up to us and asked could he help, and Vernon told him what he wanted. We followed the wizened little old man back to the men's department and began to look at shirts.

There was a soft yellow that I thought looked beautiful held up to Vernon, with his gold hair and bronze complexion. I guess the little man saw my heart in my eyes and wanted to have a little fun out of me. He grabbed a pair of men's briefs and held them up to Vernon, before we either one knew what he was doing. He said, "These would look nice on him, don't you think?" My face turned firetruck red, and I whirled around and headed for the front part of the store. Behind me I heard that dried up little old man chuckling.

Vernon paid for his purchases and took my arm as

we left the store. He won my confidence when he told me softly, "Don't let that bother you. Men have to wear underwear too." That was all that was ever said. I liked him for not teasing me.

The evening was almost over. We stopped at the drive-in for a soda. I was drinking a grapette, but I had the hardest time swallowing it. I was smitten! I thought this was the easiest man to talk with that I had ever met. He had me talking about things I liked and disliked. I even told him how sad I had felt after moving to New London.

I also learned a few things about him. He had organized a singing group called "Vernon Neely and the Rusk County Kids" and had a radio program with the group. He had been the Future Farmers of America President and loved horses and cows. He had been in service three years, and a year and a half of that time was spent in Germany. He had learned the language and spoke a little German to me. I was impressed. I liked the sound of the sweet words best. Someday, maybe he would say them to me and mean them. I hoped.

By the time Vernon delivered me to the door, I was thoroughly and completely smitten by this charming man with impeccable manners. Before I went into the house, he held my hand and asked if I would like to go riding Sunday afternoon with him and his sisters, Velma and Rose and some more friends. My heart sang a happy melody because he wanted to be with me again.

Sunday afternoon was delightful, short sleeve weather. We all took pictures and had great fun. I enjoyed the way Vernon and his sisters carried on with each other. They talked of old times and things they had done to each other; surely these girls were not talking about this mannerly, thoughtful man beside me!

That same Sunday night Vernon had a date with the girl named Jo. I knew then my dreams and happiness had been shortlived; but I would not have traded being with him for anything. That evening I went to the prayer room at church early and started pouring out my broken heart to God. I prayed while the song service was going on. I prayed while the saints testified. I prayed during the special singing, and almost all of the pastor's sermon. When he was starting to give the altar call, I got victory in my soul! I wanted to shout, dance, run tell everyone that I had just been with the Lord and I felt everything was going to be all right. How God was going to work out my life I did not know, but I had committed my all to Him. I was happy in the Lord. Jesus was now in control.

The next day I met Velma at Hunter's Drug Store to catch the bus. She was excited when she asked me, "Guess what happened last night?"

"I know," I told her, "Vernon prayed through."

"How did you know?"

Then I told her about my experience the night before in the prayer room. She had also gone to the prayer room at her church. When she came out, the Lord moved in a mighty way. Vernon had brought Jo to church with him. She knew nothing about Pentecostal worship and was a little disturbed by all the noise that was being made.

The service progressed in such a move of God that Velma had given a message in tongues and the interpretation was straight to Vernon. He jumped up and ran to the altar, forgetting all about Jo, his girlfriend. He repented right there. When the people turned to Jo, she was gone. Someone said they saw her run out the door.

I was so happy to hear the great news that I was more in the Spirit than in the natural. I thanked God all day, for my cup surely ran over. Velma had guessed that my feelings for her brother were far deeper than just a "like."

The next week we went to church and rallies. It was a perfect time of my life; Vernon loved God deeply. He had smoked, but now he chewed gum. We just enjoyed being together.

One evening we were with another couple. The young man, Joe Moore, was like Vernon's brother. He had lived with the Neely's a while because of problems in his home. We were at the drive-in cafe drinking sodas, when Joe slipped these words into the conversation: "If you all will hurry up, we will go parking." I wasn't paying that much attention to what he said. I sat my glass on the window tray and took Vernon's out of his hand and sat it beside mine. Everyone started laughing, and it dawned on me what Joe had said. I grabbed Vernon's glass and put it back into his hand like it was hot. Then I got mine and took to my corner of the car with a red neon face.

That was the week Vernon told me he was going to have to go to his grandparents in Houston to find a job. There was none to be found around New London. I was a mighty sad girl. On Saturday night, March 12, 1950, Vernon took me in his arms and kissed me; then he told me he loved me.

Vernon wrote telling me he made the trip without any trouble, and he missed me. Me! God really does answer prayer; He gives us the very best if we leave it all up to Him. Vernon said it would be two weeks before he came back home. That was the longest two weeks of my life. Everywhere I looked I saw him and he wasn't there. My heart ached to be with him.

Mollie, my sister, and I were in Overton one evening of the same week I had received my first letter. When we passed a jewelry store with a sale sign in the window, I stopped her. "Wait, Mollie, I want to go in here a minute." As I headed toward the entrance she called, "What on earth do you want to go in here for?"

"I want to buy a wedding band for Vernon."

"Buy a wedding band! He hasn't even asked you to marry him."

"Yes, I know; but he will. God gave him to me."

We looked at wedding bands. I chose a yellow gold with very little design, thinking it looked masculine. I made my purchase and left the store feeling happy inside. I also guarded that precious little box, for it represented far more than a little ring of gold.

When we got home, Mollie told Mother what I had done. Mother looked at me as if seeing me for the first time. "You can't marry Vernon. He is not our faith and he doesn't even believe in the Trinity. He believes in one God! You will have to stop going with him."

I immediately became defensive. "You told me to go pray through and God would send me a husband and now He has sent me one and you say he is not the right one. It has gone too far in my heart. Anyway, I never have believed in three Gods. There can only be two, because Jesus was conceived of the Holy Ghost."

I went to my room, closing my door behind me. I knew I had some more praying to do. I placed the box with the little band of gold in my top chest of drawers and started talking to God.

My dad finally met Vernon. Each man measured the

other and liked what they saw. From that moment on, they became friends. Daddy was not a Christian, but he was a good man and a wonderful father.

Mollie told me much later that Daddy had heard Mother tell me I was going to have to give up Vernon. He had stood in the kitchen door and said, "Lela, that is the best boy Dolores has ever brought to this house, and I think you might better leave them alone."

Mother didn't say any more to me about Vernon, but I know she was doing some praying on her own, for she was a woman of prayer and great faith. I loved her dearly and usually did what she said, but this I could not understand. When years had passed, I would know how she felt.

It seemed like everything had happened to me the two weeks Vernon was gone. I had sent my engagement ring back to my Navy boyfriend and told him there was no way I could ever marry him. He came home on leave, and a couple of days later he and a friend came to see me. My dad had to leave on a job, but the last thing he told me was, "Don't get in the car with him and go anywhere."

I told him, "Okay, I won't."

Sure enough the Navy friend wanted to go get a coke, but I told him I couldn't. I had never seen this boy mad, but he was a little upset underneath his calm. Later he was glad the engagement was broken. I received a nice letter from him in which he wrote, "I heard you were going to marry a preacher. I wish you the best."

The longest two weeks I had ever lived were finally over. It was Friday night and my Vernon was coming home. I was excited. Would he still want to go with me as much as he did? Oh, dear, a girl can think all kinds of thoughts; but when I saw him the magic was still there.

"I brought my grandparents and Sam and Edithe with me. And I would like for you to go with me to the house and meet them."

"I would love to meet them," I told him honestly, although a little nervously. I knew Sam, for he was an uncle the same age as Vernon. And I knew that Edithe was an aunt younger than either of them.

Grandmother Neely was a big-boned woman, and Grandad Neely was a slight built man. Vernon's dad took his build after his mother. He had big, beautiful blue eyes and curly eyelashes that would make any girl envious.

It was the nicest feeling to know Vernon wanted me to visit with his family and get to know them and for them to know me. One thing that really impressed me with this family was the way they loved to visit with each other. When someone suggested to Vernon's dad, "Rudolph, let's stop by the café for coffee on the way home from work," his answer would always be, "No, can't today. I have a girl waiting for me at home to have coffee and she'll have it ready when I get there."

Saturday was a lovely day. That night when Vernon came for me I was a little nervous and tried to look my best. Mollie had asked me the night before, "Did Vernon propose?"

"No, not yet," I answered. "And I do remember I bought his ring."

"What are you going to do?" she asked.

"Say yes when he asks me," I told her.

I had invited Velma, Rose and Edithe up to my house to spend the night. They would be there when I got home from our date. The Neely house had four beds, with one of them being a half; the girls had slept on the floor the night before and welcomed a bed, even though it was rather tight with three.

When I came home from our date, I fell across the bed on top of the girls and said, "I love him, I love him!" Edithe thought sure Vernon was going with a girl that had taken leave of her senses.

We went to eat in Kilgore. Sam went with a girl named Bobbie Ruth. We talked of the past two weeks happenings and about Vernon's new job with Schill Steel Company where Sam also worked. They talked of things that had happened on the job and also at church. Sam would go to church with Vernon and Grandmother Neely, but that is as far as he would go. He never made it to the altar.

As usual, I was the last one to be taken home, and we sat and talked a while.

"You wouldn't consider marrying a fella like me, would you?" He asked softly, but there was a real question in his words.

"Yes, I would," I said with a positive note in my voice.

"You really will marry me?"

"Yes, I will."

I had to tell him when I first knew I loved him. When he had smiled at me, I knew my heart was his prisoner forever. We were two people in love and everything was going to be just right for us. We knew God had worked out our lives this far. And He would work the rest from here on.

The weekend came for me to go to Houston with Mr. and Mrs. Neely. Vernon had made all of the arrangements before he went back on Sunday. I was too excited to sleep, and I kept my sister awake talking about my future. When she went to sleep, I just thought about my blond.

It was a lovely drive and I was glad to be with people like the Neelys. They were of the highest principles and character. They seemed to like me too, for which I was thankful, since I was going to be an in-law member of the family. Velma, Rose, and I were in the back seat and Sandra was in the front seat with her mother and daddy. It was a happy day for me.

We arrived in Houston before Vernon and Sam got home from work, which gave me a little time to look around, get my bearings, and calm down inside. When Vernon came in the house, he hugged everyone. Then he came over and hugged me! *"Not right here in front of everybody,"* I thought. But no one looked at us like we shouldn't. They just smiled real big. After a while Vernon took me to the tiny back bedroom and sat down on the side of the bed. He pulled me down beside him, and then reached into his pocket and took out a little blue box and handed it to me. I opened the lid very carefully and looked inside. Nestled in velvet, winking at me, was a beautiful diamond ring.

"Do you think it is all right?" Vernon asked.

"It is so beautiful! I love it!" I really wanted to throw myself into his arms and cry. I could not believe this handsome man really loved me.

He took the ring out of the box and holding my left hand, he placed his commitment on my third finger. We sat holding hands for a long time, happy just to look into each other's eyes.

When we came out of the little room, everyone was waiting and trying not to show surprise. I went to Velma and held out my hand. "Do you mind having me for a sister-in-law?"

She grabbed me and hugged me tight. "No, I don't mind. In fact I am very happy you are going to marry Vernon."

After that I showed my ring to everyone. Sam was even speechless and for once didn't tease me.

Vernon, Sam, Velma and I looked Houston over that Saturday night. Just think, a little girl from an oil field town was going to make this metropolitan city her home.

We went to Gospel Truth Pentecostal Church Sunday morning. It was Easter and they were going to have dinner in the park. Everyone was sweet. Sister Molly Lambert was especially nice. That first Sunday we became friends.

It was a good service I am sure, but I really couldn't tell you much about it. Surely the Lord has a special plan for young lovers. After we had come from the park, we had to leave for New London. I hated to say goodbye again, but it was a very happy young lady who rode home that evening.

The following Wednesday night service, Vernon was to make a talk. In his letter he wrote, "I made my talk, and Sister Lambert helped me. It was on willingness and obedience and young people's little 'no harms.' " In my mind he had done as good as any seasoned preacher could have. I was proud of him and knew he had done well.

Velma was having a hard time living with me during those weeks. I would have sudden bursts of love and pat her rather hard. Trying to find protection, she would hide from me. Oh, me, it took Velma to tell how bad it was.

Things were shaping up for the wedding. We had set the date for June 10, but found we were unable to reserve the Humble Oil Company's Recreation Hall on that night. I wrote Vernon the details stating it would have to be on June 3 or June 17, and he was to help me choose. He chose June 3.

Time passed swiftly. While my poor mother was busy with making dresses and everything else that goes on with having a wedding, I was involved with finishing out the college year. Finally, the showers, parties, dinners and decorations were done. I was to meet my love at the altar.

Walking down the aisle on the arm of my daddy to take the hand of the man with whom I was to become one, I knew God had surely chosen me especially to bless. There really are "Heaven-made marriages."

You are looking at a happy girl!

Easter 1950, engaged one day.

First Sunday Date, hoping I can hold him always.

A nice legitimate reason to touch Vernon.

Our first Sunday date, Dolores, Vernon, Velma and Rose.

Happiness is. . .

*. . .canning tomatoes
together*

By J. T. and Bessie Pugh

"Go to Bible school," my two sisters, Iva Nell and Ozella, insisted. Finding employment was always a problem for the people who lived in northwest Louisiana during the early part of 1940. Since I did not have steady employment at the time, I packed what clothes I had and went to Bible school several weeks before classes began. The campus and housing facilities of the Southern Bible and Vocational College were under construction. I was to assist with this work.

Long layovers in Shreveport and Dallas, combined with rest stops and slow speed, stretched the journey by bus over a two-day period. My spiritual commitment was very poor; selfish and personal ambitions left little or no room for God. Nevertheless, the quiet and peace of the school's rural setting comforted and stilled me. But the different lifestyle and absence of known friends brought loneliness in spite of the lavish love and acceptance I found in the family of President L. C. Reed.

Work-filled days hurried by. All too soon time for the opening semester came. Students began to arrive.

Brother Reed and I were taking care of some last minute details in one of the dormitories when the girl who was to become my wife three years later drove onto the campus in the car with her mother and younger sister, Jo.

"Sister Lula Halbrooks is a very faithful Pentecostal pioneer," Brother Reed remarked of her mother. Then, wishing to get an understanding relative to school discipline started early, he said, "I don't want you to get 'sweet' on the daughter who is being enrolled in school."

Partly because I had not gotten a good look at the young lady and partly because I wished a good relationship with the president, I assured him that I had no intention of getting involved.

Later that evening when I was introduced to Bessie Beryl Halbrooks, however, I saw that she was a very beautiful young lady. We were getting in the car enroute to a fellowship meeting when the introduction was made. Even though we rode in the same car, I sat in the front with my back to her and did not have an opportunity to either converse with her or bring her under closer scrutiny. The fact that she was a part of a singing arrangement during the service that night allowed me the privilege of studying her more closely. I remember agreeing with myself that she was very pretty!

At the time I had no intention, however, of establishing a very personal relation with any girl. But as the weeks of Bible school life flowed into months, I found myself evaluating the girls at school.

Although I turned eighteen my first year of Bible school, I had never taken a girl out on a real date. A very conservative upbringing, coupled with severe financial limitations, caused me to face all the decisions of life with a great deal of realism. Since time and money were both factors in such a relation, I reasoned with myself, *"I should not begin such activity unless I know the girl involved would make a good wife."*

I noted the good things about Bessie Halbrooks and tucked them away in my mind, without conscious effort. One of the things that first gained my attention was her steadiness and constancy. This was not only true in her spiritual life and scholastic work, but her relationships also.

I witnessed an exchange one night between her and a handsome, ladies' man of the school that I never forgot. Every girl seemed to represent a challenge to this particular young man. It seemed that all the eligible girls of the school would fall for him. Now it was Bessie's turn. I was standing near enough to hear him ask her for a date. How impressed (and I am sure how relieved) I was when she turned him down flat.

I remember thinking as I lay in bed that night, *"Here is a girl with class, character, and judgment."*

I shall never forget the day I asked her permission to escort her to an old-fashioned Sunday singing and dinner on the ground. My fellow students knew my philosophy and were quick to remind me the next day, "You said you would not date anyone unless you intend to marry them."

They tremendously enjoyed pushing me into the corner! But while they laughed, I knew deep inside that I had found the girl I wanted very much to be my wife.

One summer night, deep in the ranching and farming country of Comanche County, Texas—a little more than two years later—I asked her to be my wife.

A year later, on August 20, 1944, we were married on the same spot of ground upon which we had begun our lifelong relation three years prior.

By J. T. Pugh

My mother and Jo, my youngest sister, helped me load all my earthly possessions into the little ' 41 Ford in late September of 1941. It was sixty miles from Beattie, Texas, to Rising Star where I was to attend Southern Bible and Vocational College. I had finished high school in May and was now leaving behind some very special friends and a high school sweetheart. But upon arriving on the S.B.V.C. campus, a tinge of excitement thrilled me!

Mother and Jo helped me unload and get set up in the first room of the four-room dorm which I shared with Jimmie Mae Hogan from Carbon. It was also the kitchen and dining room for the college. Next to my room lived two sisters from Walnut Springs—Lou Ella and Gwen Rhodes. In the third room lived two more sisters from Morgan, Janette and Marine Burnet. The school cook, who also served as our matron, lived in the last room.

Mother and Jo left quickly so they could get home before too late that night; it was quite a drive over country roads.

"We're going to a fellowship meeting in Gorman tonight," someone informed me, so I got dressed and went into Gwen and Lou Ella's room to wait for Brother and Sister Reed to come for us. From their room, I could see a very handsome young man sitting on the front porch reading the evening paper while he also waited for Brother and Sister Reed.

"Say, who is this fellow?" I asked Gwen.

"Oh," she said, "that is Iva Nell Pugh's brother from Louisiana. He plans to be a lawyer."

This sounded impressive to me, but it seemed that the girls who came first already had a head start with him.

Finally, the Reeds were ready and seven or eight of us loaded into their car. At this time, I was introduced to this J. T. fellow, but I was so shy I hardly looked at him. He rode in the front seat and I sat in the back, which helped me to get a better look at him without him seeing me.

Back in those days, everybody was given an opportunity to testify, and J. T. came across with quite an impressive testimony—something about, "As the hart panteth after the water brooks, so panteth my soul after thee, O God." I thought he did sound like one would suppose a lawyer would sound. I thought he was kinda neat!

Brother and Sister Frank Martin (my pastor and wife from Suez) were there that night and when J. T. testified, Sister Martin felt in her heart that he was to be my husband. She did not tell me this, however, until some time later.

When we got back to Mountain Top after the fellowship meeting, everyone came to the dining room for fellowship and refreshments that Sister Ann had prepared. I had gone to my room. I could hear everyone talking and laughing. But there I was, too shy to come out!

Finally Gwen Rhodes (now Chapman) came after me . . .and who did I find myself seated across the table from but J. T. Pugh! He tried to make conversation with me, but I giggled and turned my attention to Gwen and Janet Burnet.

As fate would have it, the shorthand books had not as yet come in, so J. T. and I had to share a book. He would come by my room to pick up the book, and I would have a chance to say a few words to him before hurriedly slipping back into my room.

Christmas came and I went home two weeks early to work in Bibby's Variety Store during the holidays. I did not know whether J. T. was thinking about me or not, but he did make my heart skip a beat when he tried to get me not to go home. "I will pay you not to go," he said, pulling a penny out of his pocket and handing it to me. He also wrote me a card, saying (mostly) "Merry Christmas." However, I read a lot between the l-e-t-t-e-r-s!

Upon returning to school after the first of the year, I found that I enjoyed being near J. T. more and more. I set about to become good friends with his sister, Iva Nell, who was my shorthand teacher. I tried especially hard to make good grades there!

There was a lot of speculation who J. T. would ask to the end-of-the-year banquet. How excited I was when I became the lucky person (finally, the night before the banquet!). A short time later, he asked me to share the rest of his life with him.

I thought he would *never* ask my parents! He came to the farm to visit me for a few days. He helped us can tomatoes one day. As we sat around the big tub of tomatoes, I kept thinking, *"This would be such a good time for J. T. to ask Mother and Daddy for my hand in marriage."* But the conversation always went another direction.

Then one day, while he was helping Dad feed the cows, he said, "Say, what do you think of Bessie and I getting married?"

My dad was a very blunt, gruff-speaking fellow. His reply was, "Guess she is old enough to know what she's doing. . .but it means a plate off the table and not one on it."

Now that we had Dad's consent, we began to make plans for the great day.

This past forty years has been a very special time with a very special man that I feel that God made just for me!

By Bessie Pugh

Wedding Picture—taken August 20, 1944.

40th Wedding Anniversary and "Still in Love!"

The J. T. Pughs relaxing.

Happiness is. . .

...a belated
Hawaiian honeymoon

By Carole Terry

"**D**arling," my brand new husband said, "I hope you won't be disappointed in our home, but it's the best I can do for now."

He described the house as a one-room shack with dirt floors and no bathroom or running water. His dad, he said, would be living with us.

"It won't be that way for long," he apologized.

Coming from metropolitan plush, I was appalled, and began to cry. *"Oh, dear,"* I thought frantically, *"What have I got myself into?"*

But now, I'm getting ahead of the story!

When my girlfriend introduced me, a five foot, one inch seventeen-year-old who weighed a mere eighty-five pounds, to the gorgeous blond-headed, blue-eyed Chester Terry, I knew he was the one for me. The calendar leaves were torn off to August of 1966. It was the 15th.

The towering 6′ 3″ chunk of a man graciously reached out his massive hand and placed it on the back of my neck. "Want to go for a motorcycle ride?"

Icicles ran up and down my spine. Speechless, I just stared at him, then nodded, completely forgetting that my parents had a strict rule against motorcycle riding!

From that day until January 7, 1967—our wedding day—I was truly in love.

"Chester, what are your intentions with my daughter?" my dad asked on Thanksgiving Day.

"I intend to marry her," Chester replied.

"Oh. Okay!"

So my *dad* set the date: January 7.

It wasn't until after I married that I found out why he chose that particular date. He had a two-fold purpose. First, he wanted to claim me on his income tax, and second, it had been exactly one year to the date that he had his first heart attack. He wanted to celebrate that day as a "memorial" for him.

After the honeymoon of one night, we headed toward "home." Thirty miles from our destination, Chester gave me the vivid afore-mentioned description of the place. When we arrived, however, I noticed that the three-room shotgun house really *did* have floors! Though it was not elegant by any stretch of the imagination, it looked like a mansion!

"I had to run it down," he confessed, "so that when

you *did* see it, it would look like our little honeymoon cottage."

It *was* without water and a bathroom. . .and his dad *did* live with us for a few days. But I thanked God for my Girl Scout experience, and adjusted to going to the spring for water and chopping wood for the heater admirably. It was seven degrees outside and our water buckets froze over every night. It took seven quilts to keep us warm. But we were happy and in love.

In April, when the weather warmed up, we moved to California in a very over-burdened 1948 Plymouth, traveling for three days and three nights. Thirty-five miles from our goal, we broke down. I learned that one of Chester's exceptional qualities was his mechanical ability when he filed the points down right there on the sidewalk and we were on our way again.

The old Plymouth stayed in California, but we didn't. In three months time we were back in Texas with our newly acquired 1956 Chevrolet. We see-sawed between Houston and Texarkana for the next six years.

Home-building time came as he had promised. We chose New Caney, Texas, as our location. We were endowed with $200, and he spent the $200 on a radial saw.

"How in the world can we build a house with a saw and no lumber?" I asked. He was endowed with the faith; not I.

We had the decking and black paper on and were ready for the shingles. However, our pocketbook wasn't ready for shingles, so we had to wait. In the meantime, we slept under a shower curtain, awakening each rainy day with a puddle of water between us.

But love is blind! We weathered the storm, and when

our house was almost completed, Chester became restless and headed back for his native woods—northeast Texas.

By this time, we had been blessed with two children—a three-year-old son and a one-year-old daughter. We bought land and lived in a 26-foot camper for six months. History's worst ice storm hit that year, and we almost froze to death. Chester contacted pneumonia.

After that brush with illness and the elements, we started on our second home as soon as the weather permitted.

Our love added a new dimension in April of 1975. We began attending a United Pentecostal Church in Queen City, Texas. On April 20, I received the Holy Ghost and six weeks later, my husband was blessed with that spiritual gift. Praise God! Our lives made an abrupt change.

God began to bless us financially. We went into business, and I was always there supporting my companion. We were inseparable. Most of our married life has been spent in this type partnership. I seldom leave town without him; when we go, it's together.

May of 1978 is a beautiful memory. Our business surprised us with an all-expense paid trip to Hawaii—our first real honeymoon for which I had waited eleven years! Neither of us had ever flown; what a treat! Our honeymoon suite was at the Hyatt Regency with first class service, including a flower on our pillow. We strolled the beaches at night beneath a full moon, and could have been mistaken for newly-weds. In fact, the first night there, he picked me up and carried me over the threshold. We had the time of our lives!

Another change was in store for us. In September of 1979, Chester was called to preach. On our way back from national conference in Salt Lake City, Utah, we drove through a town called Gatesville, Texas. God spoke to both of us at the same time! We knew this was "our town" to start a new work for God.

In May, 1980, we purchased property, living in a small apartment "out back" and using the house for a church building. We recently dedicated a new sanctuary and live in the parsonage.

We are starting on our *third* home. "If a marriage can survive building a new home, it can survive anything," I had heard. Ours survived and we love each other more deeply than we did when we first met.

Anniversaries are special. Chester buys me a lovely gift and takes me to a very nice restaurant. We'll soon be celebrating our eighteenth—and I can hardly wait!

The camera man asked us to look up, as though looking toward our future. I never dreamed I would be a preacher's wife someday!

Car borrowed from Chester's dad for honeymoon.

Terry family.

Happiness is. . .

. . .a broken sewing machine

By Molly Thompson

My Irish Husband

"May the road rise to meet you,
May the wind be always at your back,
The sunshine warm upon your face,
The rains fall soft upon your fields,
And until we meet again
May God hold you in the palm of His hand."
                    —An Irish Blessing

At the beginning of my second term in Emmanuel Bible College, I was given the unenviable task of answering the door bell and welcoming (with a smile only) the new students who were arriving from Belfast, Northern Ireland.

The bell rang and I went, with my smile dutifully fixed, to open the door. As I did so, I was astonished to hear a rich Irish voice say, "Top 'o th' mornin' to ye, Colleen."

My first reaction was shock, as speech between men and women students was forbidden. My second reaction was indignation that a complete stranger would address me in such a manner. I was not to know that the dark-haired Irishman who swung his heavy bags through the door so effortlessly would, two years later, become my husband.

We were not allowed to work outside to earn money for our school fees. They had to be paid at the beginning of each term. We were expected to work inside the school, and it was because of this that I really got to know Bill Thompson.

My task consisted of doing the Drysdale family's sewing. Mr. Drysdale was the principal and I became very adept at patching, turning shirt collars, darning socks and frayed trouser cuffs, not to mention sewing on buttons and other small but very boring items.

I was given a small portable sewing machine to use when turning the ends of sheets to middle, and this was the instrument that brought Bill Thompson into my life. Unknown to me, he had already determined to enter it with or without my permission.

After my initial introduction to my future husband, I had studiously avoided him. How was I to know what he was thinking? There was no way *I* was going to be responsible for breaking "Rule 3"—no conversation between the men and women students. Not that I thought he would be hard to talk to, but I didn't even know his name! The list had been posted on the bulletin board, but the name, W. J. Thompson, did not register with me. I had seen the dark-haired Irishman, along with his friend several times, and was not impervious to his masculine charms; in fact, I thought he was the best looking fellow in the college. So did several other girls.

On one occasion we met briefly on the street. He had made it his business to cross the road along with his friend, Eddie Bouskill, with the obvious intention of breaking "Rule 3" (no conversation between the men and women students). Alice Davis and I were shocked to see them come over to where we were and wondered vaguely why they were doing so. As we passed on the pavement, Bill raised his hat to me and murmured, "Good afternoon." I still cannot remember if I answered or not, but when they had gone by, Alice nudged my arm and in a conspiratorial manner whispered, "Ah, Ah!"

"Don't be daft," I answered, "he was speaking to you."

"If he was," was the cryptic reply, "he's crosseyed. And another thing I'll tell you, if his intentions aren't honorable, he had no right to look at you like that"—a remark which did nothing at all to help me recover my composure.

What I did not know until after we were married was that when they had passed us, Eddie asked Bill if he knew me. "No," he replied, "but I'm going to. You see, I intend to marry her."

Completely unaware of this, I had occasion to ask Mrs. Millard, the boys' "Mother," if any of the young men possessed a screw driver, as the sewing machine which had been allotted to me insisted on coming out of the box every time I used it. It just lacked two small screws.

She told me that Brother Thompson was a joiner, as carpenters are called in England, and would surely have a screw driver among his tools. Blithely, I trotted downstairs in search of Brother Thompson, and the first person I met was Eddie Bouskill.

"Do you know Brother Thompson?" I asked him.

A peculiar expression crossed his face, and bowing with exaggerated courtesy, he replied, "You bet I do."

Puzzled by his crazy attitude, I asked him would he do me the favor of asking him to come as I needed him.

His reaction to my question left me bereft of speech.

"You bet I will, and it's happy I'll be to see his face when I do." He turned and disappeared across the patio, returning with a young man dressed in a dark blue blazer, grey flannels and white open-necked shirt, who looked at me questioningly and with a grin asked, "An' whit can a do fer ye, Colleen?"

"You. . .you are Brother Thompson?" I managed to stammer.

"Shure I am an' 'ave been fer a long time."

It was my blatant breaker of Rule 3, and I was so thankful that Alice Davis was nowhere around to see the encounter.

I managed to tell him what was needed, and we went together to the sewing room where he fixed the sewing machine. He came back every day for two weeks to repeat the process, for by his own confession, he loosened the screws every day as he left!

Three months after graduation we were married, and have lived happily ever after.

Happiness is. . .

. . .waiting in line for the bathroom

By Edith Tidrick

When I married Garvin Tidrick, I never dreamed I would have *fifty* kids!

This story begins in the little windswept, panhandle town of Dalhart, Texas, where I was born and reared. For the first nineteen years of my life, my path and Garvin's never intersected.

Then I went to work at the First National Bank of Dalhart. Immediately, I discovered that much of the conversation centered around a man named Garvin, who worked there, but was now in Dallas, Texas, where he had undergone major surgery and was not expected to live.

"He must be a very important person," I thought. *"Everyone seems to know him!"*

News of his progress spread through the bank. He had made it through surgery and had come home to recover. Later, he returned to his post of duty at the bank for half a day. Sitting propped up with a bed pillow, he dictated to me. This was my introduction to Garvin Tidrick.

All the girls were crazy about him. . .except me. I had not known him that long.

"Edith, when are you getting married?" people I had known for a long time were always asking me.

My answer was always the same: "When I can find a handsome, gentle, thoughtful, kind-hearted, lots-of-fun man!"

"Well, I guess you will never marry, since there are none of those around."

One of Garvin's cousins continually asked me, "Have you found that 'prince' you are looking for?"

"No, not yet."

"Have you considered the banker?"

"Never! I do not like him! He's too bossy as my boss; what *would* he be as a husband?"

Of course, he always carried that bit of conversation straight to Garvin. *It made for an interesting time!*

I sometimes felt that Garvin purposely kept me working late on Friday nights just because my date was waiting outside!

Eventually, we started dating—the boss and I. We went together for a year. "I fell in love with you because of your long hair, godly dress and manner," he said. As I was not Pentecostal at that time and neither was he, I have a good, strict mother to thank for that.

I came from a family of six children. One weekend, Mother and Dad left me home to babysit while they went somewhere. Garvin took me and all four of the younger children on a date and we all had a terrific time! *"That takes a good man to do that!"* I thought.

When we told my mother and dad that we wanted to get married, my dear, sweet mother said, "Why don't you wait for one year? If it's real love, it will last." Of course, we convinced her otherwise since we had gone together for one year already. She always did everything in her power to keep us children home. However, when one of us married, the in-laws then became her "kids," too, and no one had better say anything bad about them! She really loved my husband.

We moved to Ft. Worth, Texas, and both of us took positions in banks there. While working in Ft. Worth, Garvin accepted his call to preach. Upon hearing this, the bank where he was Vice President offered to pay his way to the seminary in that city at night, so that he could work in the bank in the daytime. But since he already had a college education, he declined that offer, telling me he was afraid the Lord was coming before he could get anything done for Him.

We spent two years on the evangelistic field before accepting the church in Colorado Springs, Colorado. In this beautiful city, we started out with a rented building, twelve to fifteen people (mostly children), and a lot that was about to be repossessed.

Through the years of working together, we became friends and companions as well as lovers. I had found my kind, gentle, witty, lots-of-fun man. We could laugh together, cry together, and be best of friends.

After going on a long trip with us, my mother told my sisters that she wished my dad would talk together with her like we did. "They never stopped talking the whole time," she said, "like they had not seen each other in years!" Sometimes we rode in silence and sometimes we had lots to say to each other.

I always loved children and wanted every one that I saw! As Garvin, along with his brother, was adopted by a wonderful couple, he had a special spot in his heart for every child.

A couple from our church that were out working for Sunday school found a family that did not go to church anywhere. The family had five children. It's a lengthy story, but one year around Christmas time, the courts asked us if we would take the three girls. . .and my big-hearted husband asked, "What are you going to do with the two boys?"

Upon being told that they would have to stay in a day care center, his answer was, "Bring them along. They cannot be left alone on Christmas!"

About the same time, a military man whose wife had left him with three small children was being shipped overseas, so we took those three along with the other five! We went from no children to *eight* in two weeks time. The ages ranged from seven months to fourteen years. What a difference! As one of our friends said, "Loud noises did not bother the Tidricks, but dripping faucets and little sounds drove them up the wall!"

In those days, evangelists stayed with the pastor. To put them in a motel was not hospitable. We *wanted* them to stay with us. People who dropped by our home with ten people and visitors were amazed! Those were the "good old days," days filled with laughter, tears, learning, and lots of love.

One morning with a line at the bathroom door (only one bathroom!), Garvin laughingly said, "You have to take a number!"

The "then" baby ran up and said, "Me next!"

All the other kids said, "You have to go to the end of the line."

When it was Garvin's time, she darted between his legs, saying, "Me next! Me next!"

Much laughter went up as my husband said, "It didn't work even with a number!"

My knight-in-shining-armor had it all down right. He never yelled at the kids, only telling them once and they minded him. He gave himself untiringly and with love, and they, in turn, loved him.

When he walked into the house, he never had to ask for a drink or life's little comforts. One child, "Daddy, do you want a coke. . .iced tea. . .water?" Another brought him his house shoes, another the newspaper.

The older child went to Texas Bible College. My joy was complete when she came home, sat on the foot of my bed, and told me these words that were like music to my ears: "Mom, I waited a long time, but I finally found a man like Brother Tidrick." And truly she had! Their actions, temperament, and even their looks are alike.

From eight children, our home expanded until. . . . After *fifty* foster children, I stopped counting them. We have cared for well over fifty. Some of these we adopted through the years. Some we have reared, while others came and went, but we lived to see many of them baptized in Jesus' name, filled with the Holy Ghost, and living for God. Some are married to ministers, some to managers of cleaners, shoe stores, and other business establishments. It's been fun!

In 1974, Brother Tidrick developed multimyeloma, a fast-moving form of cancer, and lived only four short months. My mother, ever a fan of this special son-in-law, was by now in her seventies, but she would drive three hundred miles to our house to see him. Upon returning to her home, she would call back to see how he was; if he was worse, back the three hundred miles she came!

She did not tell me until after he died that one time after driving the three hundred miles, she went upstairs to his bedroom and he put his arm around her and said, "Mom, I don't think I am going to make it!" That day, they had a long talk.

Before Brother Tidrick's death, we always went to church an hour early. The minute our car arrived at the front, there were young people waiting to help him out of the car and carry his briefcase in for him. All down the aisles of the church and along the front row, they would be standing to shake his hand. Being his wife, I was treated like a queen. Love radiated from him and was given back in return.

Brother Tidrick is gone now, but since his death, I have taken several more youngsters into my home. One small five-year-old boy came to me mixed up, but ten years later, he is still with me. He is now fifteen years old, handsome, and is lots of help with my little adopted seven-year-old daughter. If Brother Tidrick were alive, he would love them both dearly!

My little Mandy has cerebral palsy. God gave her to me. And does she ever keep me company! Just tonight

I told her coming home from church that she was going to get a spanking.

After a long silence, she said, "Mommy, are you still mad at me? Do you forgive me? If you forgive me, you should not give me a spanking!"

She is very intelligent. Although she is only in the second grade, she reads seventh grade material. As we were coming home recently, she asked me if it was raining at home.

"I don't know," I answered.

She bowed her head and said, "God is it raining at home?"

Total silence.

"God, I can't hear You. You're going to have to speak louder!"

There's never a dull moment with Mandy!

I am glad I found my dream of a husband, one who was willing to let me fill my heart and home with loving, laughing children.

These children and I often get together and talk about how good it is going to be when we get to the other side and are all together again.

Mandy put it all together when she said, "Mom, why don't we just go right now to be with Daddy and God?"

Her faith in God is something! Being a cripple, she told me that sometimes when she can't do something, or gets her feelings hurt, she goes into the bathroom and talks to God and "Daddy Tidrick" and that helps.

In closing this, let me say to one and all: God has been good to me. He gave me a wonderful husband and many wonderful kids. More than fifty in all. I am a grandmother many, many times now. . .besides being a mommy to

these still at home.
    "Garvin, we'll have a BIG reunion in heaven!"

Some of our beautiful girls.

Our two adopted daughters Mandy and Deanna

My very special little Mandy.

Dale, the foster son I have now.

Mandy with one of the adopted granddaughters.

Helen, one of our many "children" won an
award for our church.

My Mandy having fun.

Happiness is. . .

. . .putting God first

By Jean Urshan

When I first saw him, he was tall, thin, black eyed, wavy haired and dressed in nice clothes.

We first met in New York City. My pastor and his wife, Raymond and Dorothy Hoekstra, were invited to hold a revival meeting for Pastor A. D. Urshan. Pastor Hoekstra informed me while on our journey to New York City that Brother A. D. Urshan wanted them to bring the accordian player and singer with them to assist in the meeting. Brother A. D. Urshan had seen my picture in a publication of sermons preached by my pastor called, "In the Power of the Spirit." Brother Hoekstra said he suspected that Brother A. D. Urshan had a handsome son that he wanted me to meet, hence the invitation was extended to me.

We arrived in New York City in the fall of the year 1938, and there I met Nathaniel A. Urshan, who later became my husband.

My first impression after our very short acquaintance was that he was so good-looking that I stood no chance of his interest in me. Also, he was attending the University of Columbia and was well educated. So, I thought, why make a monkey of myself and show any interest at all? I was friendly but pretended to be very busy. I played hard to get. At the dinner table and in conversation with the Urshan family, I paid no attention to Nathaniel.

Little did I know that his dad, A. D. Urshan, was talking to Nathaniel and urging him to consider me as a girl friend.

One day Nathaniel said, "I hear you are a special singer in revival meetings." When I said that I had just come from a revival meeting in Pulley's Mill, Illinois, he replied that he didn't know there was such a place as Pulley's Mill. We had a big laugh. Then, at his request, I sang for him. After singing, I said that I had heard he had a nice voice and sang well. Then he did the singing. He sang in a rich tenor voice, "Down From His Glory."

Later, I also heard that Nathaniel had told his father that if he had any ideas about choosing this girl, Jean Habig, for his girl friend, to forget it. His dad, A. D. Urshan, told his son that he (Nathaniel) didn't have enough sound judgment to select a good companion and therefore he needed to help him make the choice.

After this uncertain and rather unique set of circumstances surrounding our first acquaintance, the revival meeting began.

There was very little interest shown between us. We both acted disinterested and aloof. Several days passed when one day I walked into my bedroom and found a bouquet of daisies. When dinner time came and we were seated around the table, I thanked whoever gave me the flowers, and then asked Nathaniel's sisters, Grace and Faith, if they gave me the flowers, since they had been so nice to me. They both answered they knew nothing about the flowers. Andy Jr., Nathaniel's youngest brother, said he thought he knew who put them in my room in a vase. With a big grin on his face, he said, "And they were bought for thirty-five cents on sale." Nathaniel, with embarrassment, hung his head and admitted he was the flower-giver.

Thus began our romance, which was to endure three years of sickness and geographical separation. Nathaniel lived in New York City and my home was Indianapolis, Indiana.

However, while in New York during the revival, Pastor Andrew D. Urshan assigned his son, Nathaniel, to be our guide and to show us some of the interesting sights of the big city.

We had some absolutely humorous times. My mother had knitted a home-made tam, which hung over to the side of my head. On windy days, the tam would be blown off my head, and Nathaniel would scramble around the sidewalks of New York and sometimes into the street to retrieve my tam. It was downright funny to watch him reach for it and have it blow further away. With disgust, he finally folded it and put it in his pocket, asking me the question, "Where did you get that thing?"

During my journey to New York City, I had taken a heavy cold. The cold had stopped up my ears and I could not hear well. When Nathaniel would talk to me, I couldn't hear what he was saying, and instead of answering him correctly, I would smile and say, "Is that right?" When what he was saying would not receive even the semblance of an answer that was in line with what he was saying, he finally said to me in loud tones, "Are you hearing what I'm saying or don't you understand English?" Again we laughed hilariously when I told him my ears were stopped up with a cold and I could not hear most of what he was saying.

Another incident interesting, but also, humorous, was when Nathaniel A. Urshan took me for a long walk in Manhattan, New York. During this lenghty trek we saw the awesome sights of the "Asphalt Jungle" called New York City.

At one point we were passing the stately Waldorf Astoria Hotel. Suddenly Nathaniel asked, "Would you like to see the beautiful lobby of this hotel?"

A country girl like me asked, "Are we allowed to go in the lobby?"

Like a typical New Yorker he answered almost majestically, "No problem!"

The lobby had a beautiful flowing fountain and canaries flying to and fro, singing, and hanging onto small tree branches planted around the lobby. It was there that he inquired into my educational background. I told him I had not finished high school. He wanted to know what kind of parents I had that did not insist on my further education. I explained that I was taken out of school because of severe sickness. At the time of my early teens I was afflicted by a rheumatic heart and Saint Vitus Dance.

From the time of our first acquaintance in New York City, our romance took a turn of uncertainty. Of course, I returned to my home in Indianapolis and the geographical difference of mileage between New York City and my home made communication difficult.

Our next meeting was in the month of May, 1939. Brother Paul and Sister Olga Box drove to Columbus, Ohio, to preach for Brother Witherspoon and Nathaniel journeyed with them. He then took the train to Indianapolis from Columbus to visit with my family and myself. This was over the Decoration Day weekend.

My mother and dad treated Nathaniel with hospitality. He had never eaten fried chicken and hot biscuits for breakfast. Mom "put on the dog," and Nathaniel lapped up everything she fed him.

Mother liked Nathaniel immediately. However, Dad was looking over this New York slicker. Of course, my dad didn't think anybody was good enough for me. In his deep voice, he said, "Keep your eye on those New Yorkers." At that time I had several suitors and Dad suggested that I give them a chance by dating them.

While Nathaniel was there, I took him to scenic Brown County in Indiana in a brand new Plymouth automobile.

I confess I had a heavy foot on the accelerator. The road to Brown County was hilly and had many hairpin curves. Nathaniel got a little green looking. He suddenly asked me to stop the car. He got out and the result of car sickness made him lose his chicken and biscuits. I got tickled and laughed out loud. He said, "It's not that funny."

His visit to our home helped to develop our interest

in each other.

In the late summer of 1939, some friends of the late Andrew Urshan were planning to visit New York City. They lived in Indianapolis, and their names were Brother and Sister Rose. They were an old German couple. They knew of my interest in Brother Andrew Urshan's son, so they suggested that Mom and I accompany them on the journey. With gladness I accepted the invitation.

It was during this visit to New York with my mother and our friends, the Roses, that Nathaniel and I began to plan for the future.

By that time Nathaniel had developed a severe chest problem and was coughing uncontrollably.

In December, 1939, Nathaniel spent two weeks in my home in Indianapolis. I was away at Apostolic Bible Institute at the time. My mother wrote and told me that Nathaniel was very ill.

After two weeks in Indianapolis, Nathaniel went to visit his grandfather and grandmother in Cochrane, Wisconsin. It was there that it was diagnosed that he was severely ill with miliary consumption which at the time was known as fast galloping tuberculosis.

Two boys who were friends of mine took me to visit Nathaniel. It was explained how sick he was and he personally told me that if he lived it would be five years before he would be well and perhaps he would be an invalid for life. This was in the days before wonder drugs like streptomycin began to make spectacular inroads into the care of tuberculosis.

Nathaniel told me then that it would be best for us to sever our engagement. In my heart and soul I could not accept this sickness as a final severance to our future plans for marriage.

Nathaniel returned to New York City where he was immediately hospitalized. I returned to Apostolic Bible Institute where I initiated periods of fasting and prayer in behalf of my precious friend.

The reports from New York, Bellevue Hospital, were very discouraging. Brother Andrew D. Urshan despaired of his boy's life. For a number of weeks Nathaniel lost physical strength and weight.

My heart was grieved and earnest prayer was made in behalf of Nathaniel. The church in New York was praying. Good friends like Arthur and Veda Witherspoon as well as Brother and Sister Norris joined me in seeking an answer for my intended.

After four months good news arrived. In April, 1940, Brother A. D. Urshan wrote that his son had a touch from the Lord. In July, Nathaniel had made such progress that they were releasing him from Bellevue Hospital. Doctors stated it was a miraculous and divine recovery. He was sent to Lake Saranac, New York, to famous Trudeau Sanitarium. There for six months he recuperated, and gained much of the weight he had lost. During that time I visited Nathaniel with a friend, Alma Beaton, to rejoice at the hand of God displayed in his healing.

In January of 1941, Nathaniel was released from the Sanitarium. His father and my parents arranged to meet in Miami, Florida, for a week of friendly fellowship. Brother A. D. Urshan was accompanied by Nathaniel. My parents, Brother and Sister Habig, chaperoned me during that visit.

Brother A. D. Urshan preached at the late Harry Geiger's church. During that time Nathaniel and I had long walks under the Miami moon. It was during these walks that we began a serious discussion of future plans of marriage.

After that romantic week, I returned to Indianapolis. The now recuperated Nathaniel Andrew Urshan began his evangelistic ministry at the age of twenty-one years. He ministered in Ironton, Portsmouth, Crooksville and New Straitsville in Ohio. It was evident the hand of God was upon his life. Everywhere he preached souls were won to the Lord.

I had the privilege of visiting several meetings Nathaniel preached. We began to sing together and join our hearts in soulwinning. In the month of April, 1941, we set our wedding date for October 1, 1941. This would take place after the Pentecostal Assemblies of Jesus Christ held their convention at Midway Tabernacle in South Bend, Indiana. The church in South Bend, was pastored by the late G. B. Rowe.

We sang nightly at that conference and the Lord favored us with Holy Ghost blessings.

On Wednesday, October 1, at Calvary Tabernacle in Indianapolis, we were joined in wedlock by three outstanding ministers: W. T. Witherspoon, Pastor R. G. Hokstra and Andrew D. Urshan. Brother Andrew Urshan in his unique way asked the audience to bless us by saying, "Hallelujah, Thank You, Jesus," and "Glory, glory!"

The anointed blessings of these men of God have followed us throughout our marriage. Calvary Tabernacle was packed with people. Many minister friends had stayed after the conference in South Bend to witness our marital vows.

The four wonderful children God gave us, Sharon Sue, Annette Ruth, Nathaniel Paul and Andrew David III, have been the joy of our lives.

All of them are now married, and from the three older children we have ten grandchildren.

Sharon Sue married Carl McKellar. Annette Ruth married Royce Elms. Nathaniel Paul married Kathy Stafford, and Andrew married Cathy Hayes.

They are all serving the Lord faithfully. When we get together for family gatherings, it is a joy to see our grandchildren singing and praising God together with their parents.

After forty-four years of ministry and years of spiritual harmony, it is awesome to look back in retrospect and marvel at the Lord's blessing.

It is absolutely true: "Seek ye first the kingdom of God, and his righteousness; and all these things shall be added unto you."

Brother Urshan and I have striven to fulfill this mission in life, putting God first. It has brought us unlimited blessings and divine privileges that we never dreamed could be ours.

This is so much like our Lord Jesus. He takes our little commitments and adds His immense blessing, and we sit back in thanksgiving to God for His "mercy that endures forever."

The Urshans' Wedding Day

Miss Jean Habig, the accordion player and singer Brother A. D. Urshan saw in Brother Hoekstra's book.

The Urshan Family, 1984. Top Row, lt. to rt. Carl McKellar, Andrew Urshan, Cathy Hayes Urshan, Kathy Stafford Urshan, Nathaniel Paul Urshan, Royce Elms. Bottom Row, lt. to rt. Sharon Urshan McKellar, Rev. and Mrs. Nathaniel Urshan, Annette Urshan Elms.

Happiness is. . .

. . .playing with paper dolls together

By Madalene Waldrep

*H*onk! Honk!

I rush to the front porch every morning when I hear the sound of the horn to wave and throw a kiss to my sweetheart as he leaves to get a newspaper.

It's been a wonderful forty years!

My daddy died when I was twelve years old, leaving Mother and me with no home, no savings, and no insurance. My six older brothers and sisters were all grown and married.

Mother and I left our hometown of Walnut Springs, Texas, and moved from place to place, living first with my oldest sister, Christine, in Dallas, then with my younger one, Rosa Lee, in Meridian.

"You have cancer. . .and you probably have about a year to live," the doctor told Mother two years after Daddy's death.

She was in and out of the hospital that entire year, and then she joined Daddy, leaving me to fend for myself at fifteen years of age.

I missed our hometown and my playmates. "Back home" memories both comforted and saddened me while Mother was ill.

I especially thought of Freddie, my childhood sweetheart, the handsome, blond-haired boy who had lived across the street from us. He had been a part of my life for as long as I could remember.

As children, we played church almost every day. He was the "preacher" and I was his "congregation." I could not recall what he talked about, only that he stood up front to deliver his sermon—and I sat on the floor and listened! Our "church" was an old truck bed that his dad had brought home. At twilight, we joined the neighborhood kids and caught lightning bugs, putting them in fruit jars. Why, he even played paper dolls with me!

"He's coming to see my sister!" I thought, deciding that my "crush" on him was fruitless. *"And besides, he talks and talks and talks to my mother."*

However, one time when I went to his house to play dominoes, he held my hand under the table! Oooooo! (I never did tell Mother about that!)

Freddie loved to eat at our house, but his mother told him, "Now son, don't eat over there! They're having a hard time!" But sometimes he just couldn't resist Mother's cooking. Daddy usually saw to it that we had meat of *some sort.* It might be opossum or turtle, but Mother could camouflage *anything* and make it taste gourmet!

One evening Freddie stood in the doorway looking longingly at Mother's biscuits (which he loved). Daddy said, "Katie, give him one of those hot biscuits and a piece of meat."

When Freddie finished eating, Daddy asked, "Do you know what you ate?"

"No, sir."

"It's ground up armadillo."

Freddie excused himself and went home!

We attended the same small school. (Of course, *everyone* in Walnut Springs attended the same school!) We frequently walked to and from school together—and sometimes he carried my books. However, when I got a head start and he tried to catch up with me, I would outrun him!

After Daddy's death and our move, Freddie joined the Navy, but we kept in contact by mail. Then after Mother became ill, Freddie wrote and asked me to marry him.

I was so excited that I was beside myself! I had no idea how to answer his letter, so I wrote back, "We can get married after the war is over."

He wrote Mother also, asking her permission to marry me. "Nothing would please me better than to have you for a son-in-law," she answered. But she was never to see Freddie again; she died a few weeks later.

Two months after Mother's death, Freddie got a leave from the service. I went to Waco to meet him at the home of his sister. He was due to arrive the following day, so

I shampooed my hair, rolled it, and donned a long red robe. In he walked, ahead of schedule! How embarrassed I was for him to see me like that! But he just hugged me, bobby pins and all!

His mother had taken me shopping for new clothes, and Freddie suggested that we go see the Methodist preacher in Iredell and make arrangements to be married. He was to wear his sailor uniform and I a navy blue dress trimmed in white.

We had little time to rehearse! The preacher took us into an adjoining room and told us what to do. No one could play the piano, so we walked in "a cappella." We stood on the wrong side of each other to repeat the wedding vows. Freddie's four-year-old niece, Nancy, watched with fascination—and repeated the vows right along with us!

After we said our "I do's," I sat on his lap for the very first time. . .right in the living room in front of everyone! Although no formal announcement was made, a lot of the townsfolk heard about our wedding and came to celebrate with us.

Freddie's Aunt Jane was in charge of the reception. It was very nice, but what I enjoyed most was the peanut butter cookies! (Remember, I was only fifteen, while Freddie was almost grown. He was twenty.)

We walked to town after the brief ceremony at 4:00 p.m. that Saturday, and one of the neighbor ladies took our picture. We had no car to go on a honeymoon, so we hired Mr. Allen Dawson to take us back to our old hometown of Walnut Springs to Freddie's grandmother's house.

As we started across town on foot to see my older

brother, we walked into a "victory rally." The big truck swarmed with people. The mayor, spotting Freddie, conscripted him onto the truck to sell peace bonds!

Upon learning that we had just married, our friends got their heads together. *"Oh, no!"* thought Freddie in a panic, *"The horse watering tank is too close for comfort!"* He slipped down from the truck and we ran to Grandma's—*fast!* In our imagination, we saw them all chasing us, with mischievous intent. Grandma turned out the lights and locked the door, calming our fears. What a blessed shelter Grandma's home was for us that night!

Freddie's thirty-day leave ended all too soon. I went with him to Dallas where he boarded the train for San Diego, California. I then went to my sister's home in Dallas, closed myself in the bedroom, fell across the bed and cried and cried like the child that I was.

Luckily, I only had to wait two months to join him. I had saved enough change to buy me a new red dress to wear on the train trip west in December of 1944. Freddie rented us a room in National City, our first "home."

We had to have groceries. When we went to the store shopping, he picked up a sack of pinto beans. "What?" I said in dismay, "You mean I have to eat those? I had to eat those at home!" (We bought the beans.)

I could not cook *anything* but cake, but we couldn't eat cake three times a day. So Freddie showed me how to make biscuits. They were not as good as Mother's, but we survived. Our first daughter, Charlotte, was born in California.

In 1946, Freddie was discharged and we returned to Texas where we purchased a dry cleaning business in our hometown. Two years later, we moved to Hillsboro where we received the Holy Ghost. We were baptized together in Lake Whitney. Very shortly, Freddie received his call to preach, and we took our first church a year later. Since then, God has helped us to start four home missions churches.

Our marriage was blessed with six lovely children—four daughters and two sons. Both of our sons, all four of our sons-in-law, and our three oldest grandsons are serving in a ministering capacity.

The law of averages was against a successful marriage for a teenager as young as I, but a strong bond of love and lively sense of humor brought us through many situations that would have otherwise resulted in chaos.

"You were probably the youngest grandmother in Pentecost," my niece remarked the other day, urging me to write "my story." I might not make the *Guinness World Book of Records,* but I *was* a young grandmother at thirty-two years of age.

Now at fifty-five, I'm a *great*-grandmother, and there's a good chance that I'll be around to ride bicycles with my *great-great*-grandchildren!

Honk! Honk!

Excuse me, I'm in a hurry to get to the front porch.

Freddie, my childhood sweetheart.

Our wedding picture October 7, 1944.

Our little family in 1959 at Eastland, Texas.

Happiness is. . .

. . .an extra scoop of ice cream

By J. O. and Mary Wallace

"Momma, do I havta," I whined. "I wanta go skating. I don't want to sit with all you old folks and talk all afternoon." But my mother insisted that talking with Momma Virden and the visiting preachers, W. M. Greer, J. W. Wallace and his son, James Onell was more lady-like than roller skating down the middle of Highway 20.

The only other thing I really remember about that first meeting with James Onell was being bored by this twenty-two-year-old young man talking about Draughon's Business College in Memphis where he was a student.

About a year later I received the Holy Ghost and Mom and I went to a Pentecostal Church, Incorporated, General

Conference in Jackson, Tennessee. A bit more grown-up now, I saw the Wallace young man running the concession stand in the basement. I hung around and then asked for a Coke. He said, "You need milk." But I bought a coke.

As he closed the stand for service, I asked, "Where are you going?"

"To the bakery to pick up more pies."

"I'll go with you," I volunteered. (I've been going with him ever since.)

I went home from that conference not nearly such a tomboy interested in skating. Sometime later I got a letter from Memphis which began my "writing ministry." I shared the letter with Mom, waited a proper two weeks, and then answered.

Very few Pentecostal boys came to Finley, a small West Tennessee village of about five hundred. Sometime later, my pastor, Brother E. E. McNatt, moved to Memphis to pastor the church that J. O. attended. It was great to visit the McNatts! After the church service the McNatts, Mom and I went by the small restaurant where J. O. worked. When I ordered ice cream, I got an extra generous scoop.

On another visit to the McNatts, J. O. invited my friend, Rebecca Edwards, and me to lunch at the Hotel Claridge. Later a group of young people went driving and another girl engineered the seating so that she got to sit by J. O. But when I complained of "cold feet," the boy I was sitting by kindly offered to change, and there I was close to that Wallace man.

World War II was spreading. J. O. felt he should leave school at Memphis and go home to be with the family.

His father, J. W. Wallace, felt a call to Nashville, Tennessee, to start a home mission work and asked his son to go with him. J. O. soon found a good job as an accountant at an oil company. Then his father and he held a tent revival on three vacant lots at 51st and Delaware in West Nashville.

That fall they moved the small congregation into a storefront. Later they decided to buy the lots on 51st street and planned to build a church. J. O. was the Sunday school superintendent with forty-two in attendance that first session in 1940.

However, his immediate plans were interrupted when Uncle Sam called and he was drafted as a conscientious objector into the Medical Corps in 1940. He left for the induction center at Fort Oglethorpe, Georgia, and for several weeks I had no address to write to him.

In Finley I faithfully wrote a letter each day and kept them in a stack on the dining table.

Jim's outfit left on a long troop train for Camp Callan, San Diego, California. When the train passed through Nashville, he could almost see his mother's house but he was not allowed to call her.

At last the day arrived when I got his Camp Callan address. Quickly I gathered all those letters, put them in a large brown envelope, ran to the post office, and mailed them air mail, special delivery. Writing really pays. He was the first soldier in his outfit to receive any mail, and not just one letter but a whole batch of letters.

We wrote faithfully each day for those two anxiety-packed years. He got a furlough after several months and came to see me.

All this time our letters, although daily, were just

friendly. I was exceedingly careful not to say one more loving word than he. I asked Mom to read my letters so that I could be sure not to be too forward.

At last came the letter when he asked, "When I come home on furlough in May for your high school graduation, will you go back to California with me?" He was stationed at an army hospital in Santa Barbara at this time.

My answer was, "How do you mean go back with you? A single girl cannot go away with a solider." This brought a more proper proposal which I answered with, "Yes, I'll be happy to marry you if my folks agree."

Well, my mother was not too sure. This was 1942 and not too many girls had gone off to marry soldiers. She said she would pray about it.

That summer, Brother A. D. Gurley held a great tent meeting at our church. He seemed very kind. I knew Papa Wallace was Brother Gurley's assistant pastor, so hesitantly I approached him. "Brother Gurley, do you think it would be all right for me to go out to California to marry Onell Wallace? Would it cause any talk or bring reproach on the church?"

"Why, Sister Mary, I don't see how it could. And I'll tell you what if I hear any such talk, I'll put a stop to it. Onell Wallace is a very fine man—one of the best."

"Momma Momma," I called as I raced home from the meeting. "Let me tell you what Brother Gurley said."

So we began to make plans. Due to the shelling of the Santa Barbara Coast by the Japanese, all furloughs were cancelled. A Tennessee wedding was out of the question. Like Rebecca of old, I would have to journey afar by train across the United States to join my beloved.

My dear father quit his job at the Dyersburg Cotton

Mill and took me to Santa Barbara. In my naivety I had no conception of the sacrifice Mom and Dad made for me. But Dad had a sister out there with whom he would stay awhile.

There was no P.C.I. or any other oneness church in Santa Barbara at the time, so J. O. and a few other soldiers were attending a small Church of the Open Door. A Greek family by the name of Cogeletas attended there. They were very hospitable to the soldiers and began to plan our wedding. It was to be in their home. They gave a lovely shower and had the reception. Their daughter, Hericula, furnished the music. A cousin who had a bakery furnished the cake. Another relative owned a florist and he furnished the flowers. J. O. had rented a small three-room apartment near the army base and Hericula and her sisters filled the cabinets with groceries from their father's grocery store.

To the young Tennessee country girl it was like a dream! A soldier friend loaned Jim a car for a brief three-day-pass honeymoon. When Jim returned to the base, his commander-in-chief notified him, "Jim, your orders have just came in. You're going to Officers Candidate School at Duke University in Durham, North Carolina."

We boarded the train to go back East. I had to return to Finley since wives were not allowed at O.C.S. However, when they insisted that Finance Officers had to train with a gun to protect the payroll, my husband, who was a conscientious objector, resigned O.C.S. and was stationed at a medical base in Ogden, Utah. For four years he was a soldier in Uncle Sam's army.

Later J. O. accepted his call to the ministry and enrolled in Bob Jones College where he studied theology. Later he attended Peabody College for Teachers.

We were married two years when our first child James Onell Wallace, Jr. was born. Five other beautiful children—Margie, Jack, Jeff, Rosemary and Joe—arrived during the next sixteen years.

God has smiled on us and we all love Him. J. O. has pastored, taught Bible school, started home mission churches, and was District Secretary of Tennessee. But most of our forty-three years together have been spent at World Evangelism Center. For almost eighteen years he served as the Sunday School Director and for seven years he has managed the Pentecostal Publishing House.

And what about me? Well, I am his helpmate! I love helping J. O. in any way I can!

J. O.'s viewpoint of a beautiful romance!

It all really began when those devoted letters from Mary Martha Hardwick started arriving. She was a very beautiful young lady back in Tennessee.

I had been drafted into Uncle Sam's army early in 1941 and hustled off to the West Coast for basic training before being sent to the Aleutian Island (Coast Artiliary Base) off the coast of Alaska. I was most interested in making that daily "mail call" assembly every time it was announced over the P.A. system.

Our first meeting was during an uneventful weekend visit at the Finley Pentecostal Church. Then, we met again during the General Conference of the Pentecostal Church, Incorporated, at Jackson, Tennessee. While this cute, young high school girl made my convention assignment more enjoyable by her help, no permanent attachment began at that point. On the occasion of my leaving for the army induction, a "farewell party" was held at the Bemis Pentecostal Church, at which time my friends lined up all the girls for a goodby kiss. Of course, this was to change before many months.

It was love through the mail, for sure! Those beautiful letters kept coming, while my reply was daily even though I had to write in the latrine after "lights out" in the evenings. I became so taken up with the great communication until it was a tremendous source of fulfillment each day. The distance of a couple of thousand miles between us was no problem to a most delightful growing love.

Since war had not yet been declared, I had a two weeks furlough all approved and signed in file awaiting the Christmas time. I really had in mind to propose to my Tennessee sweetheart on my furlough since she had promised to travel to Nashville, Tennessee, for a visit in my parents' home while I was there. Then came the news of Pearl Harbor on December 7, 1941. War was declared. All furloughs were cancelled, and no more leaves were considered. With tearful eyes, I pulled that signed furlough from the files, tore it up, and returned to the writing pad.

Six months later, after things settled down from all the war hysteria, the news came of possible furloughs for those with more than one year service. So I was on my way back to Tennessee by June. It was wedding bells for sure, but not until July 21, in Santa Barbara, California.

Although we did not have a "military wedding," it was just off the military line in a friend's home, using the post bugler to sound the wedding march. With my church and military buddies standing in,the wedding was a dream in every respect.

Mary, my bride, was a beautiful Christian girl, who has always been from that day until now, in every way, my ideal. A truly lovely person, she has more than filled the scriptural guidelines of a wife, mother and ideal companion these forty-three years. With all my heart, I am still in love!

Mary Martha Hardwick with brothers, Jimmy and Barney, about 1940.

Wedding day, July 21, 1942.

J. O. and Mary with their first child, J. O. Jr. (Jimmy was the first of four sons and two daughters.)

Courting days were few but precious!

311

Youngest son, Joe, and his bride Carla, 1983.

The Wallace family 1964, Jeff, Jack, Margie, Jimmy, Mary, J. O., Joe and Rosemary.

Fortieth Anniversary: Left to right. front row: Jack and Jenny, Jordan, Jessica; Shawn, Carey, Rosemary and Joel Edwards. Second row: Jim, Beverly, Bart, Stephanie; Alicia, Matthew, Jason, Donna and Jeff. Back row: Joe, J. O., Mary, Grandpa Hardwick, Kevin, Margie and Jerry McNall.